LEAD, FOLLOW,
OR GET ME THE
HOT SAUCE!
Cajun Wisdom to **SPICE UP** Your Leadership

Jennifer Ledet

Praise for Lead, Follow, or Get Me the Hot Sauce!

This is a fun, informative, and inspirational book, full of great ideas to enrich your life.

Brian Tracy, Author, *The Power of Charm*

Jennifer provides practical tips on fundamental skills, traits, and practices to turn learners into leaders. Credible principles seasoned with Cajun-style fun that will connect with all readers.
Dianna Booher, Author of *Communicate with Confidence* and *Creating Personal Presence: Look, Talk, Think, and Act Like a Leader*

Jennifer serves up a heaping helping of solid leadership wisdom in a giant bowl of delicious gumbo. She cleverly blends her insightful ideas on how to be a better leader using Cajun terms, stories, and – most importantly – humor to enliven her points. This is a must-read for anyone tired of old, tired, boring leadership theories. Grab a spoon and Tabasco and savor Jennifer's wonderful book.

Rebecca Morgan, CSP, CMC,
Bestselling Author of *Calming Upset Customers*

Buy this book now – highlight what you need and read it again!
Being only half-Cajun, I'm always looking for ways to fill up the missing
part of my bayou heritage. I found all of this and more in this book.
Jennifer has created the perfect recipe for leadership success – Cajun Style!
It takes a little something extra to be an effective leader and this book will
give you all the Lagniappe that you need to succeed. It's HOT Stuff!

Bruce Wilkinson, CSP, Chief Leadership Officer
Wilkinson Seminars and Presentations

Jennifer combines sound leadership guidance with a dash of Cajun spice
for a delicious recipe for excellence. She taps into her roots along the
bayous of South Louisiana to deliver a fun, engaging, and actionable
model for leadership success. An easy and insightful read for today's busy
leaders!

Don Yaeger, Leadership speaker, seven-time New York Times Best-
selling author and longtime Associate Editor, Sports Illustrated

Lead, Follow, or Get Me the Hot Sauce!
Cajun Wisdom to Spice Up Your Leadership

Cover design and internal illustrations by Lauren N. Ledet

Book design by Sue Balcer of JustYourType.biz

Sweet Olive Publishing

Printed in the United States of America

First Edition

ISBN   Print: 978-0-9852620-0-6

          Ebook: 978-0-9852620-1-3

How to order:

Lead, Follow, or Get Me the Hot Sauce!
Cajun Wisdom to Spice Up Your Leadership may be ordered directly from
www.LedetManagement.com.
Quantity discounts and customized printing (with your company's logo) are also available.
Visit us online for updates and additional articles and information.

For Steve

Thanks for helping me to keep it real, for your unwavering support in all that I do, and for reminding me of what's truly important in life.

Table of Contents

Appetizer (Prologue) 1

Get Clear on Your Assets...7

The Ingredients 9

Play Your Own Tune 15

Take Your Cue from the Cajuns.. 19

Have Your King Cake and Eat It Too 25

An Envie, an Eagle, and a Mouse 29

Beware of Blind Spots 33

Your Leadership Legacy... 37

Are You Out of Touch With Reality? 41

Lache Pas La Patate! (Don't Drop the Potato!) 45

Leadership is Caught, Not Taught... 47

Lessons from Miss Bourgeois and the Beauty Parlor............... 49

It Takes Courage to Lead 53

Dr. Jekyl and Mr. Hyde Still Show Up 57

The Lifelong Learning Journey 61

Are You Swooshing or Wedging? 65

Southern Comfort Doesn't Serve You.. 69

UNDERSTAND OTHERS TO BUILD RELATIONSHIPS.................................73

First, You Make a Roux... 75

Don't Burn the Roux! 79

How's Ya Mama 'n' 'Em? 83

Gumbo Ya Ya...87

Don't Put Strychnine in My Gumbo! 89

Tete á Tete Communication 91

Listen with Your Eyes.. 95

Get Back to Basics..99

It's Not About You...103

Modify Your Approach to Season the Conversation 107

   The Cajun Four Seasons 109

   Boudreaux and Thibodaux...113

   Autre Pays, Autre Coutume 117

   The Raconteur's Gift..121

   Some Like it Hot!..125

   Find a Neutral Ground...129

   Ask. Don't Tell. 131

   Oyster Po-Boys, Pearls, and Leadership 133

   Fired Up! Or Burnt Out? 137

   C'est La Vie 141

   Create Your Own "Bayou" GPS 145

   Just a Ti Na Na . . . or Not? 149

   Beware the 'Gators!..153

Bring Out the Best in Others with Respect 157

   The Stock..159

   Ya Gotta Be Nice to People! 163

   A Shot of Tabasco Goes a Long Way.......................................167

   A Little Lagniappe 171

   Reap a Sweet Harvest 175

   Making Wise Investments 179

   The Pierre Principle...183

   Zen-Like Leadership 187

   As the Team Turns 191

   To Get Good People to Stay, Just Ask! 195

   Crabs in a Champagne..199

   Patron Saint: A Game Plan for Leadership 203

Optimize Influence 207

   The Meaty Part..209

   Influence and Savoir Faire 213

   Coach to Win in Business, Too..217

   Super Bowl-Style Leadership 221

Ah, Duct Tape! 225

Highlighting a Tale of Two Leaders 227

The Big-Picture Aerial View 231

Feedback for Smooth Flying 235

Anchors and Bright Shiny Objects 239

Unplug to Recharge 243

Ain't Dere No More 247

Mardi Gras, Lent, and Leadership 251

Cajun Revival! 255

Epilogue: Laissez Faire 259

About the Author 262

Acknowledgments 263

Endnotes 264

Get Clear on Your Assets
("The Ingredients")

 Understand Others to Build Relationships
("The Roux")

 Modify Your Approach to Season the Conversation
("The Cajun Four Seasons")

 Bring Out the Best in Others with Respect
("The Stock")

 Optimize Influence
("The Meaty Part")

Appetizer (Prologue)

Cajun people are known for their rich culture, abundance of delicious, flavorful foods, spirited music, plenty of good friends and family, and of course, the *joie de vivre* (love of life) of its people.

The people of South Louisiana are like no other in the world. Having gone through devastating hurricanes, economic downturns, and a damaging oil spill, they are the model for resiliency and enduring spirit.

I never intended to write this book. Well, not in this way—not with a "Cajun flavor." Sure, I'm from South Louisiana—a town called Thibodaux located along the banks of Bayou Lafourche, also known as bayou country or Cajun country; I'm fond of calling it God's Country.

Having worked for many years in human resources, I held leadership roles in both the public and private sectors, overseeing the work of hundreds of employees. For the past 14 years or so, in my consulting practice, I have worked with clients and organizations in a wide variety of industries. In each of these experiences, I have witnessed first-hand the importance of having excellent people skills in leadership—and in all facets of business success.

"But what does a book on leadership have to do with the Cajun culture?" you might ask. Well, let me back up a bit here.

After providing leadership development coaching and consulting for several years, I began speaking professionally on these topics. Colleagues and friends in the New Orleans and Baton

Rouge areas—as well as friends and fellow members of the National Speakers Association (NSA) all over the country—encouraged me every step of the way. (I also have lifelong friends who think it's hilarious that I get paid to speak. They know me, and they know I'm gonna talk whether I'm getting paid or not!)

This old Cajun saying still holds true: "No two gumbos are alike… and nobody's gumbo's as good as ya mama's!"

One day, a friend and fellow speaker I respect "called me out" as we sipped coffee at a local café. (No, it definitely was *not* a Starbucks. We have terrific local coffee shops in South Louisiana. Not that there's anything *wrong* with Starbucks. Just sayin'. . . .)

Anyway, my friend confronted me by saying that the minute I took the platform to speak, I became some "other being" on stage. That person lacked my personality, my wit, and even my accent. I guess I had become *honte* or embarrassed about my Cajun background and way of speaking. I worried that if I spoke with my natural accent, my IQ would plummet 20 points in the minds of audience members and they'd look down on me.

I'll never forget how my friend chided me by saying, "Jen, people want to hear *you* speak, not some generic imitation of a professional speaker! Be yourself, accent and all."

At that point, I decided to embrace my bayou roots and pour that Cajun flavor into my message. (Footnote: Just for the record, while Mama was born and raised in Thibodaux, my daddy was born in Florida, so technically I'm not a full-blooded, *vrai* Cajun. But having lived here for almost 60 years, Daddy always called himself a "naturalized" Cajun. His accent was the same as everybody else's and I think he used more Cajun expressions than Mama. Because the Cajuns, or Acadians, intermarried with the French, Spanish, Germans, and others once they arrived here in Louisiana hundreds of years ago, many who call themselves Cajun have no blood connection to the Acadians. That's okay. It's all good.)

Leaders everywhere can all take a page from the playbook of the Cajuns. This book tells you how.

A Staple of Life

"In other parts of the world, little girls are made of sugar and spice and everything nice, while little boys are made of snips and snails and puppy dog tails. Little Cajun children, on the other hand, are made of gumbo, boudin, and sauce piquante, crawfish stew and oreilles de cochon."[1]

In the bayous of South Louisiana, gumbo is a staple of our lives. As you likely know, this thick Cajun soup is prepared with whatever ingredients are readily available. We might have (in the vocal cadence, like "Bubba Gump") seafood gumbo, chicken and andouille (sausage) gumbo, shrimp okra gumbo, filet gumbo . . . and the list goes on.

Gumbo is also the ultimate comfort food to Cajuns. When Louisiana has its first "cool snap" (when the mercury drops just below 70 degrees), you'll likely hear someone say, "Ooh mae, this is some good gumbo weather!"

Suffice it to say that those who were raised in Cajun country were spoon-fed gumbo as toddlers. Heck, I was probably given gumbo juice in my baby bottle! As a result, we all have a preferred gumbo recipe.

This old Cajun saying still holds true: "No two gumbos are alike . . . and nobody's gumbo's as good as ya mama's!" In fact, in my family, if I'm cooking, we're having seafood gumbo. But if my husband is cooking, we're having chicken andouille gumbo. And look, I wouldn't dream of treading on his turf—nor he on mine. We each stick to our own gumbo and never the twain shall meet!

Contrary to popular belief gained from the television show

Swamp People, the Cajuns are not all alligator hunters, nor do we run around in the swamps yelling "Choot 'em! Choot 'em!" Rather, Cajuns are fun-loving, generous people who enjoy a unique way of life along the river, the bayous, the prairies, and the swamps of Louisiana. Our one-of-a-kind culture both charms and intrigues outsiders; our fierce determination helps us withstand the inevitable challenges that have come our way.

> *Just like your signature gumbo recipe, the insights you glean will come through your unique experiences and become exclusively your own flavor, or style.*

Leadership *is* a kind of gumbo; you add a little of this and a little of that; you bring your distinctive flavor and style to it. However, the main steps/ingredients to making every kind of gumbo are the same. Even though your leadership style is unique, throughout this book you'll gain a greater understanding of core principles that will strengthen the base ingredients for your success.

Step into my kitchen and I'll share my favorite gumbo recipe with you. While we're at it, I'm eager to share my GUMBO recipe for Great Leadership.

How to "Cook" with *Lead, Follow, or Get Me the Hot Sauce!*

You probably know that the people skills essential in your recipe for success can be both expanded and applied in your day-to-day work experience. This book helps you do that.

Now, I understand you'll naturally be eager to get to the *eating* part of the recipe, but fixing the GUMBO comes first. I encourage you to go through each step—GUMBO— because each is necessary to creating a delectable dish.

Through relevant stories, anecdotes, and examples, the skills and qualities of successful leaders will come out—like the spices flavoring a gumbo. As you read each of them, I challenge you to ask, "So what? What does this mean for me? How can I apply this in my work, my life, and in my relationships?" From there, you personalize your takeaway ideas and mix them into your own leadership style.

Just like your signature gumbo recipe, the insights you glean will come through your unique experiences and become exclusively your own flavor, or style.

Adding a Pinch of *Lagniappe*

Lagniappe is a Cajun term meaning "a little something extra." In the true Cajun tradition, I'm excited to provide you with a little something extra. So throughout the book, you'll notice that I've sprinkled a little *lagniappe* signified by a hot sauce bottle. These segments will direct you to an online resource that will help you "spice" up your leadership.

As you read, pretend you and I are sitting on my porch having a strong cup of *café au lait* and a lively conversation. I'm serving you a short, bite-sized nugget you can easily digest and apply in your real-world circumstances.

In addition to sitting on my porch, I invite you to log into my blog at www.LedetManagement.com and join in the conversation. There, you can post comments, pose questions, and ask for advice for improving your specific flavor of leadership.

Mae cher, I hope to see ya'll there soon!

Let's cook up a GUMBO full of leadership lessons from the bayou.

Get Clear on Your Assets (The Ingredients)

The Ingredients

The Cajun people always seem to be cooking, eating, talking about what they're going to cook, or bragging about what they cooked last night. You'll hear expressions like, "Talk about good!" and "Mae, it was so good, it'd make ya wanna slap ya mama!"

The Cajuns are even known for their penchant to talk about what they're gonna cook for supper before they've gotten up from the dinner table. (Oh and by the way, in South Louisiana, there is no such thing as lunch—only din-

Before any Cajun Mama (or Cajun Daddy, for that matter!) can decide what she'll cook, she takes stock of what she's got on hand.

ner and supper. I believe this comes from the French or Acadian word *souper*, which is the evening meal.) We do love to cook—and that's because we love to eat! Like they say, "Cajuns don't eat to live; they live to eat!"

Before any Cajun Mama (or Cajun Daddy, for that matter!) can decide what she'll cook, she takes stock of what she's got on hand.

In South Louisiana, we are blessed to have abundant natural resources. We live along the bayous, the Mississippi River, and the Gulf Coast, the prairies, and the swamps. At any given time, we may have on hand beautiful gulf shrimp, fresh *sac-a-lait* or speckled trout filets, salty oysters or fat blue crabs, smoky andouille or spicy boudin (sausage), and always bountiful fresh vegetables from the garden.

Naturally, to decide what I'm going to cook, I need to assess what I have on hand. As you develop your own leadership style or "recipe," you won't want to skip this important first step of taking stock either.

Begin by looking *within* to assess your;

- strengths,

- interests,

- talents,

- personality,

- skills,

- aptitudes, and

- behavioral tendencies.

Why is this self-assessment so important? Well, we know that people who successfully connect with others—whether in a sales, customer service, teamwork, or leadership capacity—have certain characteristics in common. They are:

- self-awareness,

- self-confidence,

- self-discipline,

- high emotional intelligence quotient, or EQ, and

- ability to adapt to different situations and people

Do you notice a theme? Yes, these characteristics all begin with self-evaluation. Self-awareness often gets overlooked by those seeking to be successful leaders, but because it's a key ingredient, it can never be skipped.

Have You Taken Stock of Your Strengths and Weaknesses?

Have you identified and do you clearly understand your strengths, your gifts, your talents? Are you also aware of your limitations, sometimes referred to as weaknesses?

In my workshops, I see the difficulty some individuals have identifying their strengths and gifts. Exploring the reason for this, I've concluded it's because of common conditioning. Generally, people are taught to focus more on areas where they're weak and address those, rather than building on areas where they're strong.

No self-respecting Cajun would throw out leftover food. Rather, they'd get the most out of every asset.

They've also been cautioned to be humble, to not *vanter* as we'd say in South Louisiana—that is, avoid being braggadocios and downplay their talents.

Humility is certainly an admired quality for a leader. But most people fail to see that being humble doesn't have to mean—and should *not* mean—downplaying the talents and assets that make them unique.

If you've been coached to improve in your areas of weakness, it's easy to forget all about your strengths. Marcus Buckingham and others have written extensively about this tendency and have created what's called the Strengths Movement.[2] (You can learn about this trend by reading Buckingham's books and by exploring other experts who write on this subject.)

In my coaching, consulting, and leadership development work, I see many people "sleepwalking" through life totally unaware of the effect they have on others. Indeed, they have no clue how their actions are perceived by those around them. As I coach them through the process of becoming more self-aware, I can see the "I get it" light going on over their heads. Suddenly, they understand why they think, act, and feel the way they do. They also gain a better sense of how they come across to others and how people look at them.

To take stock of your assets, you can tap into many instruments that help you understand yourself and your behavioral style, your strengths, your personality, and your skills. I encourage you to take as much time as you need to get clear on your assets. You'll be a better leader because of it.

Wasting Your Assets

A good Cajun cook doesn't allow even the smallest amount of leftovers to go to waste. Take, for instance, one of my favorite breakfast foods, *pain perdue,* or as folks in other parts of the country would say, French toast. *Pain perdue* originated as a tasty way to use up stale bread.

No self-respecting Cajun would throw out leftover food. Rather, they'd get the most out of every asset. In the same way, having a clear picture of your strengths and assets will enable you to put them to work rather than waste them. With greater awareness, you'll be able to determine how you best contribute to your team, to your organization, and to others in your life.

You can purposefully set yourself up for success by giving the best you've got to give. But you can't do that by minimizing or downplaying your strengths. Instead, center your actions around your strengths and continue to spice them up, build on them, highlight them, maximize them. Why is this important? So you can become:

- more insightful as you develop your own leadership style,

- more acutely aware of what others see in you and believe about you, and

- more conscious of how you engage with people, never again sleepwalking through your interactions.

Successful leadership, like successful Cajun cooking, requires taking stock of the assets/ingredients you already have on hand.

Play Your Own Tune

In no other place can you find such top-notch entertainment, delectable food, and beautiful outdoor experiences, as well as the most diverse music, than at a Louisiana festival. With the state of Louisiana playing host to more than 400 festivals each year, it's no wonder our area is known as the Festival Capital of America.

I once heard it said that all the festivals in the state are named after a fruit, vegetable, grain, insect, or animal. Here, we celebrate every crop harvested, every delicious indigenous dish cooked, every variety of plant and wildlife native to our area. And of course we revel in our music! Louisiana is the birthplace and home of a wide range of diverse music styles such as Zydeco, Jazz, Blues, Swamp Pop, Gospel, Dixieland Brass, Congo, Salsa, Country, Rock, Reggae, and Ragtime, just to name a few!

Whether you're jazzing it up, singing the blues, or marching (or dancing) to the beat of a different drummer, strive to find the music inside you.

Louisiana also boasts an abundance of talented musicians who have honored the music inside them, honed their talent, and made a conscious decision to play their own tune.

To be successful in leadership—or anything else—you have to play your own tune. Whether you're jazzing it up, singing the blues, or marching (or dancing) to the beat of a different drummer, strive to find the music inside you. As playwright Oscar Wilde once said in his witty style: *Be yourself; everyone else is already taken.*

What does playing your own tune have to do with effective leadership?

Until you're clear about who *you* are and feel comfortable in your own skin, you simply won't have the self-assuredness to relate well with others. And being a leader is *all* about building relationships that influence action. It all must come together harmoniously.

Notes for Playing

I've composed a few notes of my own to show how you can play your own tune.

Identify and embrace a distinctive style that reflects who you are. Before you connect with others, connect with *yourself*. You can't be yourself if you don't know, understand, and accept your unique qualities first. So as suggested earlier, take time to identify your strengths and assets. Did you know people put more time and effort into planning their next vacation or selecting a flat-screen TV than into knowing themselves better?

To thine own self be true. You are both the composer and the conductor of your own song. So know your values and identify which ones are non-negotiable. Don't try to be someone you're not in an attempt to impress others (like I did when I began speaking professionally). Instead, assess what makes up the essence of who you are and magnify it.

No one is sure who said it or when, but this saying rings true loud and clear: *If you don't stand for something, you'll fall for anything.*

When in doubt, leave it out. These words of wisdom from Mrs. Stafford, my elementary school band teacher, have resonated with me ever since the fifth grade. But what should you leave out?

Well, how about self-criticism, for one? I'm willing to bet you are your own worst critic. Sure, you've played wrong notes and made mistakes. You're not alone. (Remind me to tell you about my bassoon solo in the high school concert band!) Bring the lesson into your soul, then move on.

Actually, the only folly in making a mistake is not learning from it. You can also leave out any tendency to compare yourself to others—something that often leads to resentment. And you can't fully play your own tune if you're full of resentment.

Rest, relax, reflect. In any musical composition, the silence between the notes is just as important as the notes themselves. To be effective, give yourself and others (your listeners) space to absorb what comes between the notes. Take the time to rest, relax, and reflect. Ask, "What's working for me and what isn't working?"

While you're reflecting, don't take yourself too seriously. Instead, find space for laughing at your goof ups. With their never-ending supply of Boudreaux and Thibodaux jokes, Cajuns love laughing at themselves all the time!

Laissez Les Bon Temps Roulez! The main chord that runs throughout our diverse Louisiana music is letting the good times roll. That means constantly choosing to enjoy being with your fellow musicians as you play the tune that's yours to play.

In Louisiana, you'll never exhaust the supply of diverse music available for your listening (and dancing) pleasure. And regardless of your style preferences—both in music and in life—you can always play your own tune.

Take Your Cue from the Cajuns

To understand the Cajun culture and the way of life in South Louisiana, you must first understand its rich history. The Cajun story is one of determination, struggle, resilience, and triumph.

The roots of Cajun culture go back to Nova Scotia, Canada, where French travelers settled nearly 400 years ago. For a century, they lived quiet, simple lives in their remote village of Acadie. They were virtually isolated from the rest of the world, surviving as farmers, trappers, and fishermen.

In 1755, during the French and Indian War, the British expelled them from their homes, imprisoned some of them, forced others onto ships bound for English colonies and prisons, and then burned their villages. (This is often referred to as the *Grand Derangement*.) Families were separated as thousands of Acadians were scattered all over North America, the Caribbean, France, and England.

In 1764, the Spanish, who controlled the vast Louisiana territory, sent word that the Acadians would be welcome in Louisiana. (The Spanish wanted to populate the area with people other than English!) The Acadians saw this as an opportunity to be reunited and again nurture their culture.

Once in Louisiana, the Acadians found themselves adapting to a new land—*and* to a new rule three times. Louisiana went from Spanish rule to French, and then to American rule. The Acadians, or "Cajuns" as they became known, adjusted to their new homeland,

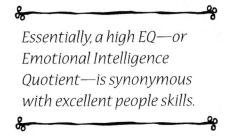

Essentially, a high EQ—or Emotional Intelligence Quotient—is synonymous with excellent people skills.

surviving by farming, trapping, and fishing, albeit in a different climate and with different crops and wildlife than they'd known before. Yet they kept their culture alive and once again became isolated for another century, essentially freezing their language from further evolution.

Ironically, the Cajuns succeeded in preserving their culture by blending with other cultures. The French and Spanish influenced the Cajun culture, as did the Germans and Africans. These hardy people knew who they were, but by remaining inclusive instead of exclusive, they were able to develop and flourish.[3 4]

The same principle holds true in business and in life.

Best Predictor of Success

What one characteristic is the greatest predictor of a person's success as a leader, manager, or supervisor in the workplace, in personal relationships, in the community, in the home, and even in religious groups? No, it's not IQ nor any particular technical ability. It's not accounting skills or reasoning skills, nor is it a person's ability to speed read or win at computer solitaire.

Although all of these skills can come in handy under certain circumstances, none of them can predict overall success like a person's Emotional Intelligence Quotient (often referred to as EQ or EI).

Yep, that's right, EQ. Who knew?

Given the many definitions of EQ, I prefer this one: "Emotional intelligence is the innate potential to feel, use, communicate, recognize, remember, describe, identify, learn from, manage, understand and explain emotions."[5] Essentially, a high EQ—or Emotional Intelligence Quotient—is synonymous with excellent people skills.

You can see examples of this every day—like the brilliant, well-educated man with the "alphabet soup" behind his name who struggles to communicate with other humanoids, while the person who has neither degrees nor exceptional intelligence quickly climbs to the top of the ladder of success.

This we know. Wherever you stand on that ladder, improving your emotional intelligence can positively affect your ability to interact with others. *Every* people-oriented job requires high EQ to enjoy a high level of success. For example, a sales professional needs the ability to gauge a customer's mood and buying style, and then know which product to pitch as well as when to back off. A team member requires good people skills to interact successfully with co-workers, superiors, and customers.

Certainly because leaders have a lot of influence on a lot of people, high doses of EQ are essential for success.

Technically Brilliant But . . .

Take Bob as an example. Bob is a manager with a large widget manufacturing company (names have been changed to protect the guilty). Everyone who knows Bob recognizes his technical brilliance. His thorough understanding of his business's and his industry's technology are unmatched. Plus his ability to strategize and assess risk make him a valuable asset to his organization.

But (and you could see that "but" coming) when Bob interacts with people, he comes across like sandpaper—abrasive, demanding, harsh, and at times, sarcastic. He makes the brashness of Rosie O'Donnell look like the calm of Mother Teresa!

No doubt you know others like Bob. These people just can't seem to connect to other humans, which makes working with them a challenge. The worst part? They have no clue how they come across to others. Their bad behaviors fall into their blind spots.

What Bob needs (no, not a swift kick in the pants although it's tempting) is a strong shot of emotional intelligence—a higher EQ. Thankfully, emotional intelligence (unlike the intelligence of IQ) can be learned, developed, and enhanced. If Bob is willing to learn and practice, he can find empathy for others, speak to them respectfully, and stay open to their input in workplace interactions.

What does Bob's example mean for you as a leader? You can certainly benefit from a booster shot in your people skills. Increasingly more organizations are recognizing an unequivocal need for higher EQ at work. It's no longer a place typically considered to be more "head" than "heart."

First Step in Improving Your EQ

Ironically, the first step to understanding others is to understand yourself. Increasing self-awareness actually helps you improve your interpersonal skills and even see your own blind spots. Yes, regardless of the make and model of the car you drive, you (and everyone else) have areas that can block your view of yourself!

In addition to knowing yourself, as a leader you play a key role in your organization's success by directing the efforts of others and acknowledging their accomplishments. To be effective, you have to know what makes them "tick." Like the Cajuns, by remaining open—by being inclusive instead of exclusive—you can become more successful with people.

When you tap into the power of behavioral styles in your leadership, you'll see dramatically improved employee morale, lower turnover rates, and increased productivity.

In my leadership and teambuilding classes, participants use tools that help them identify and understand the behavioral styles of others. When you tap into the power of behavioral styles in your leadership, you'll see dramatically improved employee morale, lower turnover rates, and increased productivity. Most important, you'll see a shift in your approach toward team members. That shift will hugely affect your ability to influence their performance.

Today the Cajun culture is alive and well with vibrant music, art, and food but only because these joyful, resilient people were confident in their own identity and open to others. Can you take a cue from the Cajuns?

Here is the kicker: Developing your own EQ can dramatically deepen your work relationships, increase your chances for promotion, boost your ability to influence others' productivity, and—because of these shifts—improve your organization's bottom line!

Have Your King Cake and Eat It Too

In South Louisiana, we go straight from the hectic holiday time of Christmas and New Year's right into the Mardi Gras season. It begins on January 6, also known as Twelfth Night and continues until the day before Ash Wednesday, also known as Fat Tuesday, or Mardi Gras.

It's said the tradition of King Cake at Mardi Gras time came to South Louisiana with the first French settlers, making its first public appearance for the Twelfth Night Revelers Ball in 1871. Regardless of when or how it began, it's a delicious tradition that I, for one, am glad has endured through the decades.

The delicious Danish-style King Cake is laced with cinnamon and decorated in the Mardi Gras colors of purple, green, and gold. Traditionally, Mardi Gras crews (often spelled "krewes") placed a golden bean in the King Cake and the young lady who found the bean in her piece of cake was named their queen. In later years, instead of a bean, bakers hid a small plastic baby in each King Cake. Nowadays, people enjoy King Cakes throughout the entire Mardi Gras season. The person who gets the

You wouldn't think that finding a hidden plastic trinket in a cake would be a big deal or that people would consider it a hugely desired treasure, but at Mardi Gras time they do.

piece with the baby is expected to bring the King Cake to the next party.

You wouldn't think that finding a hidden plastic trinket in a cake would be a big deal or that people would consider it a hugely desired treasure, but at Mardi Gras time they do.

Unearthing Hidden Treasures

I love the idea of finding treasures hidden within. I believe everyone has a "treasure" buried deep inside (and no, I'm not referring to a golden bean or a plastic baby). I'm fortunate I was able to unearth my own hidden treasure a few years ago.

I remember my "I get it" moment in September, 2004. It was like an "aha moment" you hear described on the Oprah Winfrey Show. From that point on—without meaning to sound too dramatic—my life has never been the same. After that point, I completely changed the focus and purpose of my business and felt more enthusiasm and passion for my work. Even my personal relationships improved. (No, I didn't suddenly become skinnier, sexier, or even get whiter teeth; my transformation was cooler than any of these!)

When did this life-changing moment come? During a training program when I did a self-assessment process that took me "within" to unearth the strengths, assets, and gifts I never realized I had.

While at this program, I suddenly understood why I think, act, and feel the way I do. It was as though I'd been looking at myself in a fogged mirror and it suddenly cleared. This time, I wasn't concentrating on all the icky unattractive faults and bumps and lumps I normally focus on. Instead, I was seeing the "good stuff" I could bring to my work and my relationships. Truly eye-opening.

At that point, I knew I had to share similar insights with others so they'd experience the rewards that I have. Best of all, I love teaching what I learned that day, which is this: *By going within, you can* identify your own strengths, interests, values, skills, tendencies, preferences, and more.

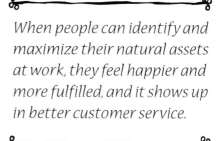

When people can identify and maximize their natural assets at work, they feel happier and more fulfilled, and it shows up in better customer service.

Shortly after, I shifted my business from human resources consulting to providing leadership development and team-building programs. In these programs, I emphasize self-awareness as a first step to personal and professional growth—as well as one of the essential ingredients in leadership GUMBO.

Have *you* taken time to discover your hidden treasures? Have you identified where you can make your best contribution to your team and organization? Do you fully understand what you do best? Can you leverage your strengths to benefit all?

Why Care About Self-awareness?

Studies show that 83 percent of people who score high in self-awareness are also top performers within their organizations.[6] Clearly, the two go hand in hand. Truly successful leaders—those who are highly respected and admired and who attract loyal team members—almost always have a solid understanding of their own strengths and limitations.

In your quest for self-awareness, I suggest you become a detective and spend as much time as necessary getting to know yourself. Identify your limitations as well as your strengths—your hidden treasures. You may be delighted at what you find!

Unearthing my own hidden treasure allowed me to shift the focus of my business so I could fully capitalize on my strengths. Before this epiphany, I plodded through my work, rarely excited or energized by it. I simply wasn't making the most of my greatest gifts.

Since my discovery, though, I realized that, not only do I enjoy my work more, but I'm providing a greater degree of value to my clients and their organizations. Around me, I see this happening again and again. When people can identify and maximize their natural assets at work, they feel happier and more fulfilled, and it shows up in better customer service. Best of all, they adopt a more positive attitude—and *that* affects productivity and profits.

So set up a win-win. Have your King Cake and eat it too. Seek the treasures hidden within and strive to maximize them for your own joy, happiness, and success!

An Envie, an Eagle, and a Mouse

The French term *envie* means a craving or a hankering for, or to feel like doing something. It's a term commonly used in South Louisiana, most often about a type of food. Such as "Ooh, mae, I have an *envie* for some boiled crawfish!" (Which is true for me, but sadly, I have to wait for crawfish season!)

What do you have an *envie* for? As a leader, do you have clarity about what you want to achieve? Have you spelled out what you want to accomplish?

Not only do great leaders get clear on their goals and their vision for the future, they *desire* them with passion, enthusiasm, and energy—like my *envie* for crawfish! I recently saw a slogan for the state of Louisiana that said "Louisiana: Pick Your Passion!"[7] The results of a recent *Science Magazine* poll show that Louisiana is America's happiest state. Although I'm not surprised, I'm thrilled to see that my assumptions are validated. The people of Louisiana, and particularly South Louisiana, are passionate people. This label is certainly in keeping with our laughing way of life, our *joie de vivre* and unique culture.

How can you learn from the Cajuns and apply this approach in your work as a leader? Once you pick your passion and you get clear on what you want, that vision becomes a powerful force that pulls you forward. Then, like all great leaders, you'll be able to

Effective leaders have eagle vision and sharply focus on the big picture, on what lies ahead, on what they're working toward.

share your vision and enlist team members on your quest.

The Sioux Indians regard the eagle as a symbol of great vision because of its ability to see distant vistas with immense clarity. The mouse, on the other hand, represents the tendency to focus only on what's immediately in front of us because this small animal explores only its immediate surroundings with its nose, eyes, whiskers, and paws.

Do you relate to the mouse to a certain degree? Most people do because it's easy to get caught up in "mouse" vision when life gets so "bizzy" it can make you dizzy. (Hence, my newly coined word "bizzy.") Dozens of pressing, urgent tasks demand time and attention so, in a mouse-like manner, you focus only on what's in front of you.

By comparison, effective leaders have eagle vision and sharply focus on the big picture, on what lies ahead, on what they're working toward. Although they too have daily "to-do" lists, they keep their long-term aspirations front and center. They take strategic action steps each day, week, and month to move them closer to their goals.

What's the Key to Eagle Vision?

Many people have goals for their organizations or for their teams but not for themselves. Business philosopher and motivational speaker extraordinaire, Jim Rohn, often said, "You should work harder on yourself than you do on your job." He suggests that as you invest in your personal and professional development—as you advance toward your goals—your organization and team benefit, too. Collateral benefits, if you will.

So know what you crave—your *envie*. Identify your passions, unexplored interests, curiosities, and dreams. When you pinpoint and clarify the goals you have for yourself and your career, you're on your way to becoming a great leader.

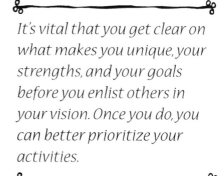

It's vital that you get clear on what makes you unique, your strengths, and your goals before you enlist others in your vision. Once you do, you can better prioritize your activities.

Make your goals explicit, inspiring, and congruent with who you are and what you believe in. Be specific and strategic about the future you envision for yourself and for your team. Continually ask, "Is what I'm doing congruent or contradictory to who I am? Have I clearly defined my beliefs, values, and purpose?" If your work doesn't align with who you are, no doubt you'll have little enthusiasm, engagement, or excitement for it. (Believe me, I feel your pain. I've been there.)

It's vital that you get clear on what makes you unique, your strengths, and your goals before you enlist others in your vision. Once you do, you can better prioritize your activities. Instead of focusing on what's right in front of your nose or paws or whiskers, aim to develop your far-reaching eagle vision.

What do you have an *envie* for? Once you know your passion, get clear on your eagle vision and then share it with others on your team and in your organization.

Oh, and by the way, if your *envie* is for crawfish, you'd better get in line—behind me!

Beware of Blind Spots

Thibodaux, the small town in which I was born and raised and I reside today, is nestled on the banks of Bayou Lafourche in the parish of Lafourche. (In Louisiana, thanks to our French and Spanish heritage and predominantly Catholic roots, we have parishes instead of counties.) It's a quaint town with many residents earning their living in sugarcane farming or the oil and gas industry. Picture moss-draped oaks and a generally slower pace of life than in the city.

I can remember my daddy teaching me how to drive my VW Beetle (stick shift) on a deserted old cane field road. I guess he figured I couldn't hurt anyone; there was virtually no traffic except for a farmer on a tractor every once in a while. Finally, once he felt confident that I was as good as I was going to get, he allowed me to *roder*—to run the roads in town, go to my friends' houses, and go to school. But it was a long time before I was allowed to drive out of town or—*Mon Dieu!*—to the city.

As I was growing up, any time plans were made to go to New Orleans, we would say we were going to "the city." But going to New Orleans meant driving on the Interstate and, even though I eventually lived there for many years, my daddy never felt confident about me driving on the busy Interstate!

Blind Spots

Speaking of driving on the Interstate . . . have you ever been driving down the Interstate when you attempted to change lanes and narrowly missed hitting another vehicle? Suddenly you realize you didn't even SEE the other vehicle! It must've been in your *blind spot*. You might have blind spots in your work relationships, too. I'm referring to those behaviors you do *unconsciously*. Your co-workers, team members, and even customers may be conscious of them, but you're completely unaware of how you're coming across to them.

> *It's like looking at yourself in one of those (dreaded) three-way department store mirrors. You get the complete view from every angle.*

Warning: Blind spots can be detrimental to building positive relationships.

Why should you care about building positive relationships, you might ask? Research shows that a full 85 percent of the success you experience as a leader—and in life—is determined by the quality of relationships you cultivate with others.

Conclusion: Building relationships is pretty darned important to your success!

After studying and working with successful leaders for years, I've found they have critical skills in common—including self-awareness. That means they understand themselves, their strengths, their limitations. They also know how they come across to team members, subordinates, superiors, and customers. Because of that awareness, they lead consciously—NO blind spots.

How Can You Change Your Blind Spots?

In my work coaching and training leaders, the first step in all of my programs is to have leaders complete a behavioral self-assessment—a tool that lets them see themselves as others see them, often for the first time. It's like looking at yourself in one of those (dreaded) three-way department store mirrors. You get the complete view from every angle. (Who invented those mirrors anyway?)

I recently worked with executives and directors of a large international construction firm. As they came into the meeting room, it felt as though I could cut the tension with a knife. Even after we went through the self-assessment process, the strain remained. When they discussed the way they came across to others and their perceptions, the CEO all but shouted "Eureka!" Then he openly confessed he had no idea how his behaviors had been affecting his leadership team and the organization as a whole.

If you have no idea how you're coming across to others, then ask team members for their honest perceptions. Listen to what they say with an open mind and a non-defensive attitude.

He admitted that, in his quest to grow the business, he'd often been inconsiderate and even rude. His results-oriented, demanding, and impersonal approach had created divisiveness and competition among the directors, preventing him from building positive, trusted relationships. As a result, the company culture was one of tension, dissension, and distrust.

If you were to do an assessment, what blind spots would show up?

Do you intimidate others?

Do you lack focus and attention?

Do you fail to make vital decisions?

Do you overanalyze and lose sight of how the people involved are affected?

Whatever your blind spots may be, I urge you to identify them and work on improving in those areas. If you have no idea how you're coming across to others, then ask team members for their honest perceptions. Listen to what they say with an open mind and a non-defensive attitude. Then identify those behaviors you want to address.

Unless you want to continue driving down those deserted cane field roads, you need to adjust your mirrors and get rid of the blind spots. Build positive relationships, improve communication skills, and become an effective leader by looking at yourself in the three-way mirror—from ALL angles.

Your Leadership Legacy

Louisiana has given the world some colorful characters, legends in their own right. From Louis Armstrong and Fats Domino to Huey Long and Edwin Edwards, to Bryant Gumbel and Harry Connick, Jr., we have talented, interesting folks who have left (and are leaving) powerful legacies behind.

Identify individual qualities you'd like to be known for. This becomes a list of core values akin to a personal mission statement.

Political analysts and historians study U.S. presidents, their administrations, and their tenures, analyzing their contributions and downfalls after they've left office. They spell out the legacies they'll leave for posterity. Ultimately, they help shape how people will view each president's legacy.

What's Your Desired Legacy?

Let's pretend for a moment that the "administration" you lead will be analyzed in a similar fashion. What will your legacy be? What will people remember about you and your tenure in office as a leader?

Do you like what you predict your legacy to be? If not, great

Describe the leadership legacy you and your "administration" want to leave, then commit to beginning your actions toward that end today. Start with the end in mind.

news! It's not too late to change it. Stephen Covey (of *The 7 Habits of Highly Effective People* fame) advocates beginning with the end in mind. So determine your desired endpoint. Figure out what you'd *like* others to say about you after you're gone. And begin making that vision come true today.

Remember as a kid you'd ask your friends, "So what do you want to be when you grow up?" This exercise is similar. Depending on your age, you may believe it's too late to think about what you want to be, do, or have when you "grow up." But I know it's never too late to become the kind of person/leader you've always wanted to be.

Start now. Make a list of how you'd like to be remembered as a leader (as a father, friend, mom, sister, spouse, etc.). Identify individual qualities you'd like to be known for. This becomes a list of core values akin to a personal mission statement. Consider your beliefs, values, interests, passions, and dreams. Let your imagination run wild!

Don't stress; if need be, you can change what you wrote later. I'm not saying you'll *need* to alter the list. Rather, I encourage you to be creative—and don't worry about being realistic right now. (Okay, in my case, at 5 feet 2½ inches tall, I probably wouldn't list my desire to be a pro basketball star, but that doesn't mean you shouldn't be wildly imaginative.)

On your list, leave space between each quality/characteristic you write. Then once you've completed your list, go back and consider what actions you'd need to begin today to create this legacy. Plan action steps to take each month, week, and day to bring yourself closer to your vision—and follow through on your plan.

For example, if you'd like to be remembered for being a good listener, list three ways you could practice. You might state that when someone approaches you and wants to talk, you'll stop what you're doing, make eye contact, and practice active listening.

You might also write down you want to get into the habit of "asking" more and "telling" less. That means posing well-thought-out questions and listening carefully to the answers. You get the picture.

For this exercise, write down the actions, habits, and behaviors you can take to get you where you want to go. Then incorporate these habits into your daily routine, weaving them into your inter-actions with others. You might even post reminders where you can see them, lest you ever forget your resolutions/goals.

Like me, perhaps you don't have the skills or attributes to be the next pro basketball star. But you *can* be the leader, father, friend, mom, sister, spouse you want to be.

Describe the leadership legacy you and your "administration" want to leave, then commit to beginning your actions toward that end today. Start with the end in mind.

Are You Out of Touch With Reality?

I have a confession to make. Here, lean in closer. I don't want just anybody to hear this.

I have never watched a reality television show!

You heard me right. I've never witnessed one airing of *American Idol*, never dialed up *Dancing With the Stars*, and never tuned in to one episode of *The Bachelor/Bachelorette*, or even one installment of *America's Got Talent*.

Not that there's anything wrong with those programs. Reality TV has just never interested me.

UNTIL, that is, I caught a snippet (on the national TV news) of *Undercover Boss*. This reality show features the CEO of a prominent company who goes undercover as a new employee in his/her company. The CEO-turned-entry-level-employee gets to experience the effects of his/her leadership and company policies firsthand.

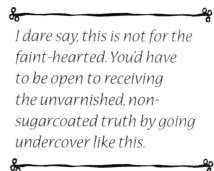

I dare say, this is not for the faint-hearted. You'd have to be open to receiving the unvarnished, non-sugarcoated truth by going undercover like this.

This concept really piqued my interest, so I went online and watched two episodes—all in the name of professional research, of course. And I learned a lot, once I got past the fact that a cameraman follows these people and records their every interaction (they tell the "real" employees they are documenting the experiences of new employees). It's quite revealing.

What Would *You* Find?

I wonder, as a leader, if you'd ever go undercover in a similar manner. And if you did, what would you find? What do your employees think of your leadership style? Your policies and procedures? The company culture and environment you have created?

I dare say, this is not for the faint-hearted. You'd have to be open to receiving the unvarnished, non-sugarcoated truth by going undercover like this. You see, many of these bosses on TV discovered how unrealistic their policies were among their people. Some were floored by the level of dedication and loyalty expressed by employees in the lowest ranks of the organization. Most were moved to make changes in their leadership practices.

Have you created an environment of respect and trust? Do team members feel comfortable disagreeing with you for the greater good of the company or the customer? Or are your employees walking around afraid to mention that, ahem, the emperor (aka YOU) has no clothes?

It can feel intimidating to ask for candid feedback from your team members and direct reports, peers, and superiors. It's like (ladies, you'll appreciate this analogy) here in South Louisiana when I am getting ready to go to a party, or to the grocery store, or to just about anywhere, I first go to the mirror and *ponponer* (primp). I make sure my hair is fixed and lipstick applied. Of course, I want to take a hand mirror and check out the rear view to make sure I don't have a rat's nest in the back of my hair! When I *ponponer*, I want to be sure to get a complete view from every angle.

See Yourself in the Rear View

As a leader, looking at that view can be a powerful experience. Seeing yourself from every angle—including from the perspective of your team members—can even move you to change.

It's common for policies, procedures, rules, and regulations to be put into place without giving much thought to how they'll be implemented, whom they'll affect, and whether they're practical or even necessary. Yet self-aware, confident, secure leaders aren't threatened by dissenting opinions. And they wouldn't put in place a procedure without considering its frontline implications and applications.

> *Yet self-aware, confident, secure leaders aren't threatened by dissenting opinions. And they wouldn't put in place a procedure without considering its frontline implications and applications.*

So, go ahead and *ponponer*, but be sure to check out the rear view! I challenge you to get up from behind that desk to mix and mingle with the rank and file in your organization. Ask for—and carefully listen to—the input you receive.

Without a cameraman recording every interaction, you'll find out about *their* realities. They might be quite revealing!

Lache Pas La Patate! (Don't Drop the Potato!)

This old Cajun adage is often quoted but maybe less often understood. A modern-day translation might read something like "Hang in there!" or "Finish strong!"

The Cajun people and the people of South Louisiana have certainly endured tough times—numerous hurricanes, economic downturns, a damaging oil spill, and more. But we're bouncing back better than ever.

I believe this resiliency reflects the suffering and persecution of the Cajuns who lived through the *Grand Derangement* when they were exiled from Nova Scotia. Today, the saying *lache pas la patate* has become a testament to the resiliency and enduring spirit of the Cajun people.

As a leader, you can take a page from the Cajuns' *lache pas la patate* playbook by emphasizing these characteristics:

- **Values.** Cajuns are known for their strong family and community values. During difficult times, everyone comes together and helps each other. In the face of adversity in your business, organization, or industry, do you hold firmly to the values and beliefs that got you where you are? Don't compromise them!

- **Courage.** Someone *has* to make the courageous decisions. After all, making inconvenient, uncomfortable, and unpopular decisions are why you're paid "big bucks." Do you bury your head in the sand or grab the

bull by the horns? Remember that by making no decision, you are, in effect, making a decision.

- **Integrity.** Integrity and trust form the foundation of
  great leadership. If people believe they can't trust you
  in one area, then they can't (and won't) trust you at all.
  Are you doing what you say you'll do and fulfilling your
  commitments?

- **Commitment.** In good times and bad, your team needs
  a committed leader who won't throw in the towel.
  Obviously. But your team also needs a leader who won't
  waver, doubt, or question the mission and purpose of the
  organization and his or her role within the organization.
  Are you constantly flirting with second thoughts, or are
  you holding firm to your mission?

- **Optimism.** Like the Cajun people, great leaders deal
  in hope and optimism. People believe that you're in the
  know. If you spout gloom and doom instead of projecting
  optimism about the future, people will assume that you
  have a good reason for being negative. Yes, your attitude
  has a tremendous effect on those around you. What
  kind of outlook—pessimistic or optimistic—are you
  presenting?

- *Joie de vivre* **(love of life).** Cajuns need no excuse for a
  party. It's this spirit of fun, lightheartedness, and *joie de
  vivre* that gets 'em through the tough times with their
  sanity intact. Are you creating an environment that's
  serious, even melancholy or miserable? Or have you
  set up one of camaraderie and celebration that people
  enjoy? Remember, you set the tone—for better or worse.

Yes, once you know the story of the remarkable Cajuns, you
understand their indomitable spirit and ability to not just cope but
thrive through challenging times. How can you *lache pas la patate*?

Leadership is Caught, Not Taught

"A picture is worth a thousand words."

"Practice what you preach."

"Actions speak louder than words."

"Example isn't the main thing in influencing others. It's the only thing."

"What you're doing speaks so loudly, I can't hear what you're saying."

Hundreds of quotations like that illustrate the same principle—your actions, behaviors, even gestures, make powerful impressions on others.

One exercise I use in my leadership development programs drives this point home perfectly. I ask everyone to make a "circle" with their thumb and forefinger (like an "okay" sign). I then tell them to bring their circle up to their cheek. As I say this, I bring my circle up to my chin. What happens? Nine people out of ten follow my actions rather than my words. They touch their chins!

*Frankly, it's not enough to tell your team members what to do. You have to walk your talk and **show** them in congruent ways.*

Similarly, you set the standard as a leader who influences followers by your actions. You're held to a high standard. You set the tone for what is and is not acceptable in the workplace. Frankly, it's not enough to tell your team members what to do. You have to walk your talk and *show* them in congruent ways.

People Follow Your Actions First

You see, as the exercise demonstrated, when your actions don't match your words, people follow your actions. The same holds true in relationships such as parenting. When my teenagers started driving, imagine their rolled eyes if I told them to buckle up every time they got in the car but didn't do it myself!

I recently volunteered at my son's high school for a program called Challenge Day. It's a day designed to end bullying and teasing while breaking down false facades that kids (and adults) put up. The theme for this day came from what Gandhi said: "Be the change you wish to see in the world."

What a powerful message, one that resonated with the teachers and parent volunteers as much as it did with the students. And it resonates for business people as well. Mark Miller, VP of Chick-fil-A, put it this way: "Much more of leadership is caught than taught."

The lesson? People watch how you act more carefully than they listen to what you say. Always walk your talk.

Lessons from Miss Bourgeois and the Beauty Parlor

When I was young, I *hated* Tuesday afternoons. That's because Tuesday was the day Mama went to the beauty parlor. (To some of ya'll, the beauty parlor might be called the hair dresser or the salon, but to us here in South Louisiana, it's the beauty parlor.) Anyway, on Tuesdays, I had no choice but to mope along to the beauty parlor.

But that changed when I was in the fourth grade. That's when my teacher Miss Bourgeois started getting her hair done on Tuesdays as well. And I *loved* Miss Bourgeois!

But one Tuesday at the beauty parlor, I was complete-

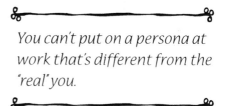

You can't put on a persona at work that's different from the "real" you.

ly shocked to see Miss Bourgeois *smoking cigarettes*. Now, the fact that she was smoking in the beauty parlor wasn't that shocking; heck, in those days of prevalent smoking, doctors probably puffed on cigarettes as they delivered babies!

What shocked me was that Miss Bourgeois smoked at all. It seemed so out of character for her. And to make matters more confusing, she talked differently to the ladies in the beauty parlor than she did to her fourth-grade students. She seemed, well, different there.

I have to be honest; finding that out crushed me. It was as though she was being "fake" with us in the classroom and "real" with the ladies at the beauty parlor. I didn't know the word "inauthentic" then, but that's how it felt.

As an adult looking back, I now realize Miss Bourgeois was being quite professional in the classroom and simply letting her hair down at the beauty parlor (pun intended). To be a successful leader, though, I think people need to see *who you really are* all the time. You can't put on a persona at work that's different from the "real" you. Being authentic isn't optional.

Having All the Answers

A coaching client believed his team would only respect him if he had *all* of the answers *all* of the time, *un person qui sait tout.* In his mind, if he exposed any limitations, he'd not only lose respect, but he'd be seen as weak and mousy.

Of course, he didn't have all of the answers all of the time so he bluffed and faked and fudged. That behavior eventually caught up with him. Ultimately, he realized 'tis better to be *real* than to be *right.*

The axiom *fake it till you make it* does not apply to leadership. However, many axioms have rung true and they've helped me a lot. I'm a big believer in the following axioms because they express authenticity so well.

The *Encarta Dictionary* defines authentic as "not false or copied; genuine and original, as opposed to being a fake or reproduction." Authenticity in leadership is about being genuine, which means you don't have to be Superman/Superwoman (nor should you try) to earn the respect of those on your team.

- "He who knows others is learned; he who knows himself is wise." – Lao Tzu

- "To thine own self be true." – Shakespeare from *Hamlet*

- "Do not wish to be anything but what you are, and try to be that perfectly." – St. Francis de Sales

Be Super YOU

Instead of being Super Man or Super Woman, be Super YOU. To earn the respect of others, simply be the best *you* YOU can be. And know that, unlike what my client believed, you won't have all of the answers all of the time.

Also know that's okay. By admitting your limitations, you may actually empower others. But trying to fudge or fake who you are results in people not trusting you.

If you want to influence others and effectively lead them, first effectively lead yourself. Let your hair down. Besides, when you try to fake it, people (even fourth-graders) see right through you.

> *By admitting your limitations, you may actually empower others. But trying to fudge or fake who you are results in people not trusting you.*

Authentic leadership is more about who you are than what you know. If you depend on your knowledge and expertise for your team's respect, you'll be sunk the first time you encounter a challenging situation.

Instead, be the kind of leader who is honest and real, who admits not knowing all the answers, but who will strive to find the solutions.

Are you relaxing with your team members? Are you admitting your limitations? Success is about being trustworthy and letting people know who you are . . . authentically.

It Takes Courage to Lead

I recently posted a question on Facebook asking friends what they think is the most important characteristic of great leaders (a highly scientific and validated poll!). The answers ran the gamut from honesty and integrity to fairness and fun.

But one quality that kept popping up intrigued me the most. Courage. Here in South Louisiana, we might call it *sans peur et sans reproche*, or without fear. In fact, many deemed courage to be *the* one most important quality of a great leader.

Nando's Story of Courage

A few years ago, I had the privilege of hearing Nando Parado speak at a National Speakers Association conference. While you might not recognize his name, you may recall his story. And what a story it is!

In 1972, a charter plane carrying Nando's Uruguayan rugby team and a few family members crashed deep in the remote, snowy mountains of the Andes. For 72 days, the world assumed all those on board had died. But several survivors endured unimaginable hunger and cold (many had never seen snow before and most wore only t-shirts, jeans, and flip flops) and even survived an avalanche. They stayed alive by resorting to cannibalism.

Nando, after recovering from a severe head injury and learning that both his mother and sister had died, assumed a leadership role among the survivors. No one assigned this role to him or gave him a title. Instead, he saw a need and stepped up.

Consequently, young Nando (only 22 at the time) decided not to stay at the crash site and wait indefinitely to be found—or starve to death. With his teammate Roberto, he set off to find help—no going back. While he knew they might die making the trek, at least they would die going for help for all of them. The two hiked for 10 days until they finally came across a Chilean farmer who summoned those who eventually rescued them.

I was especially struck by his unbelievable will to live and, like others hearing his story, asked, "Would I have had a fraction of Nando's courage in a similar situation?"

The story of Nando Parrado has fascinated me since I heard it as a young girl. Listening to him tell it in person and with visuals moved me to tears. I was especially struck by his unbelievable will to live and, like others hearing his story, asked, "Would I have had a fraction of Nando's courage in a similar situation?"

Courage Tops the List

Yes, to be an effective leader, courage tops the list. As some of my Facebook responders pointed out, a leader must find the nerve to make the tough decisions. I think that too often leaders are afraid to make and implement decisions that might render them unpopular with their team members.

But leadership is not a popularity contest. We can get lots of input and take many factors into consideration, but when it comes down to it, an effective leader makes decisions based on what's in the best interest of the organization *and* its people.

As a leader, Nando made many decisions his teammates didn't

like. Yet he stood out for finding the courage to hike out for help. Great leaders won't ask another person to do what they're not willing to do themselves; they willingly go first.

I'm not sure if all great leaders have *sans peur et sans reproche* (no fear). I do know this: young Nando Parrado modeled exemplary leadership qualities—and continues to do so today by telling his story.

Dr. Jekyl and Mr. Hyde Still Show Up

What kind of leadership brand are you creating? "But I'm not a product. Heck, I don't even have a personal logo. Why would I have a brand?" you might be protesting.

I respectfully disagree, *mon amie*. No, I'm not a marketing expert, but I do play one on TV. Er, seriously, I have read enough books on marketing to know that your brand is not a logo or a slogan. Rather, your brand is *what you've become known for*. And yes, as a leader

> Studies show that having an inconsistent boss detrimentally affects productivity. (Big surprise, right?)

you have a brand, whether you realize it or not. In fact, you're creating your leadership brand every single day. And although you may not be conscious of the image you're projecting, the people around you are highly aware.

Knowing What You're Known For

Call it what you want—your reputation, your style, your trademark. I see it as your brand, which is determined by how you'd answer these questions:

- What are you known for?

- How do you show up each day?

- Do you come to work in an upbeat, supportive mood one day, but then snap people's heads off the next?

From these few questions, you see that your brand is what people experience and expect from you. Successful leaders know that *consistency* in displaying that brand is key. If you ask your team members to describe your brand and they shrug their shoulders and say "*Je ne sais quoi*" ("I don't know" or "it's hard to describe"), then you need to get to work on it.

More important than showing up is HOW you show up and whether the same "you" shows up consistently from one day to the next.

For people to feel secure and thus be productive, they need to know the same rules apply day in and day out. They also need to know which "you" will show up. As the Cajuns would say, *bon a savoir* (it's good to know). When team members can't predict how you'll behave, react, and respond from one day to the next, they feel as though they're walking on eggshells—off-balance and unsure of themselves. Their praiseworthy idea today might be cause for a chewing out tomorrow.

Studies show that having an inconsistent boss detrimentally affects productivity. (Big surprise, right?) Need I point out that when people feel like they're on thin ice because they don't know what will set off their boss, they're prone to having accidents, making errors, suffering on-the-job injuries, and providing suboptimum customer service.

Suffice it to say that when a key leader displays a Dr. Jekyl and Mr. Hyde personality, profits and productivity suffer.

Become Consciously Aware of Your Brand

In a previous job of mine back in the day, the manager of a neighboring department resembled the Dr. Jekyl/Mr. Hyde dichotomy to perfection. *Pauvre bêtes!* The poor people who worked with him constantly showed nervousness and jitters lest they set him off. Their regular morning ritual was first to determine which persona had shown up that day, and then to adjust their behaviors accordingly. About the only thing they could count on was his consistent inconsistency! Many talented people passed through that department; few stayed for long. The stress he created in the environment pushed them away.

> *More important than showing up is HOW you show up and whether the same "you" shows up consistently from one day to the next.*

Think about the lost productivity, the poor morale, the missed opportunities for creativity and innovation. Think about the potential lost customers, too—all due to the erratic behaviors of this one manager.

Woody Allen once said that 80 percent of life is showing up. I disagree. More important than showing up is HOW you show up and whether the same "you" shows up consistently from one day to the next.

Think about what kind of leadership brand you are creating. Right now. Today. Are you known to be a loose cannon that goes off at the slightest provocation, or are you known to be a rock-solid, dependable supporter of your people?

The Lifelong Learning Journey

In South Louisiana, folks are—shall we say—a bit *gaga* about college football. Regardless of whether you're from South Louisiana and support Louisiana State University (LSU), I'm willing to bet you're gaga about some football team. I once heard you can't find any men on the streets anywhere in South Louisiana on a weekend; they're all either at the hunting camp or at a football game.

Recently, we packed up our son for college, moving him into the dorms at LSU. Other than anticipating the football games and extreme partying, he seemed pretty blasé about the whole thing. Then again, I guess that's typical for a teenage boy. I, on the other hand, was bouncing off the walls with excitement.

My friends couldn't believe I didn't get teary sending my "baby" off to college. Truth be known, I'm jealous! I've always loved learning new things and even though it's not really cool to love school when you're 18, I actually did. Okay, I didn't always go to class back then (don't tell my kids that). But to this day, I love to expand my mind with new ideas.

Did you know that you can never exhaust your capacity to learn? What an amazing concept! Despite a belief you might have about limited amounts of gray matter, your brain can always make room for new learning.

More than that, as a leader (or aspiring leader) within your organization, you have a responsibility to continue your own professional development. That said, don't look at it as an *obligation*. Like going to college, you can view your development as an exciting journey with lots of twists, turns, and detours—especially if you're open to learning new concepts and exploring exotic lands.

Multiple Forms of Learning

Although I am a card-carrying bookaholic, I know not everyone shares my love of reading. (Blasphemy!) You don't have to read a lot of books to continue your learning journey. Your method can take many forms.

For example, you might—

- attend training courses, seminars, and workshops.

- participate in certification programs through your professional organizations/industry.

- attend conferences and trade shows sponsored by professional organizations.

- go to lectures or presentations offered by local universities or community colleges.

- join a book club in your neighborhood or at your local library or bookstore.

- create or join a mastermind group of like-minded professionals.

- network with people within your industry, especially those above your level.

- attend industry-specific professional meetings and events.

- listen to audio books and programs in your car and/ or during your commute to and from work or client meetings, etc.

- seek out and sign up for e-learning webinars or teleseminars. (I especially like teleseminars I can load onto my iPod for later listening. Yes, I am a nerd.)

As a leader, one of your goals should be to create a workplace with a development culture, one in which employees are given opportunities to learn new skills. Support and encourage your team members to continue their own development. And by participating in professional development programs yourself, you not only learn new skills, you model this practice for those in your circle.

> *You don't have to read a lot of books to continue your learning journey. Your method can take many forms.*

Great leadership takes constant effort. That includes the effort to continually work at learning; it's part of your job. As John F. Kennedy once said, "Leadership and learning are indispensable to each other."

In today's knowledge-based business environment, people spend a good portion of their workday learning. In fact, anyone unwilling to continue learning gets left in the dust of those who do make the effort. I see it everywhere. To remain competitive today, learning, growing, and developing is essential. Otherwise, you'll be plodding along in your horse and buggy as your competitors speed past you in racecars.

Managers Deserve Support

Given the tremendous importance of a supervisor's role, you'd think companies would do everything possible to develop and support their management employees. Not so. Obviously, something's got to change.

In today's highly competitive market, companies must get the most productivity they can from every employee. Therefore,

> *Great leadership takes constant effort. That includes the effort to continually work at learning; it's part of your job. As John F. Kennedy once said, "Leadership and learning are indispensable to each other."*

paying attention to managers—the biggest contributor to employee productivity—is a priority.

Many of my one-day and half-day workshops for a company's managers are held in-house. They provide a golden opportunity for managers to get together, exchange ideas, network, and realize they're not alone in the problems they face. They also learn from others' experiences, often saving themselves hassles down the road.

Remember, your ability to learn new things can never be taken away from you. Improving your knowledge and skills increases your value to your organization. And especially in uncertain times, who wouldn't want to increase their value to the organization?

Treat professional development as an exciting lifelong journey that's even better than going to college. Enjoy the scenery, the side trips, and the souvenirs along the way.

Are You Swooshing or Wedging?

Who are you? Where are you going?

Deep, thought-provoking questions, right? I looked at these questions on a huge banner hanging in our high school main hall every school day. Decades later, I still ponder them.

Who are *you*? And where are *you* going?

Such questions remind me of this Yogi Berra saying: "If you don't know where you're going, you might end up someplace else."

Now, I won't get into the mechanics of goal setting here—plenty of resources can help you with that. But let's talk about the importance of challenging yourself beyond the boundaries of what you think you can accomplish. That's how to get to the core of who you are and where you want to go!

In my world—and probably yours—now is no time for complacency. Tough economic times require individuals in organizations to be proactive and adaptable, to offer creative solutions to help build and maintain a competitive edge. That means you're required to push yourself beyond your current comfort zone. No time to kick back, sip your *café au lait* and eat beignets.

Beyond the Comfort Zone

Speaking of being outside my comfort zone, my family and I recently enjoyed a ski vacation in Angel Fire, New Mexico. As you can imagine, a bayou girl from South Louisiana doesn't see much snow, let alone get much practice skiing. The closest we have to a White Christmas on the bayou is a once-in-every-10-years snow flurry in which the flakes pretty much melt before they hit the ground. Maybe once in every 20 years it'll be cold enough for the snow to last for a few hours and we can make a tiny snowman *or* have a snowball fight, but we don't have enough snow to do both!

So picture a bunch of Cajuns packing up an RV for the long, arduous drive to New Mexico. And I do mean it was an arduous drive! A bunch of *cooyons* (fools) from the bayou have no clue how to drive on icy, snowy roads, nor how to use snow chains. But we were prepared. We brought large pots of gumbo we'd cooked ahead of time, lots of our beloved Community Coffee, and an adequate supply of adult beverages to enjoy in our chalet on the mountainside.

On the slopes, despite a few glitches due to ill-fitting boots, I managed to improve my technique skiing down the beginner runs. In fact, I felt a huge sense of accomplishment at having conquered them.

But I knew I needed to shoot for bigger, loftier goals.

As I pushed myself to tackle the intermediate slopes, I experienced fear, reluctance, and a longing for my good ole comfortable beginner slopes. Yet I knew they'd become boring, and besides, it's embarrassing to have your kids swoosh past you while you wedge all the way down doing your best impression of a pizza pie!

Eventually, with persistence and the patience of friends, I became adept on the advanced slopes. By the last day, I felt exhilarated and proud. Confident as a pro, I did my own version of *swooshing* down the mountain. (Don't look for me on the medal stand at the Olympics, though.)

Complacency—the Enemy of Excellence

If you want world-class results, you have to willingly step outside of your comfort zone and challenge yourself. Seek new situations, learn new skills, swoosh down new mountains, even master the Rubik's Cube. In leadership and in life, complacency is the enemy of excellence.

That's who you are! A master pushing yourself to swoosh down the advanced slopes of life.

As a leader, team member, or sales professional, you can't afford to cautiously wedge your way down the easy slopes in this current business climate. Use this time to get everyone trained (yourself included). Freshen your skill sets, adopt new strategies, and get more organized than ever before.

Then, when the economy and your business take off, you'll be poised for success, swooshing down the slopes to your desired destination. And have your bowl of steaming gumbo ready to enjoy when you get there!

Southern Comfort Doesn't Serve You

You probably already know your preferred ways of doing things. Your days flow more smoothly, and you feel less stressed and hassled when you can spend most of your time doing what comes naturally—just hanging out in your comfort zone.

While in the "zone," you happily do things you like and do them the way you prefer. Ideally, no one and nothing interrupts your flow.

But recall when you've had to do something that took you outside of your comfort zone—perhaps a new assignment or different job responsibilities. How did it feel? A little off-kilter perhaps?

My friend Denise told me how she'd been called on to shoulder different responsibilities at work. She felt totally uncomfortable for a while. She had to think on her feet and be innovative in crafting solutions. She had to put forth more effort and "bust her can" to achieve what she wanted. She certainly couldn't just chill out in her comfort zone.

But as a result, Denise felt more fulfilled and rewarded than ever for her efforts. Her confidence soared as she approached her work with a sense of rejuvenation and enthusiasm.

That can happen for you when you step out of your comfort zone.

Growing Pains

Over the past few years, as our sons became teenagers, we visited the doctor on more than one occasion due to pains in their legs and knees. Fortunately, each time the doctor assured us nothing was wrong; the boys were just experiencing growing pains. Apparently, they were growing so fast, their tendons and ligaments couldn't keep up. (Not surprisingly, my grocery budget couldn't keep up with them either!) To help the pain, the doctor encouraged them to stretch before playing sports to stay limber, but the discomfort, he reassured us, came from their growth spurts.

> *Stop all of the depressing water cooler chatter and encourage team members to get uncomfortable. Allow them opportunities to grow and stretch.*

As I have strived to grow my business, I've experienced those growing pains and *lived full time* in my *discomfort* zone. At times, I long for the good ole days when I could just do the "same ole, same ole" (which might actually mean "same ole lame ole"). But to reach new heights, I realize I have to endure those "growing pains" like my sons did.

You know the old saying—*What got you here won't get you there* (also the title of a best-selling book by Marshall Goldsmith[8]). The message? Get too comfortable and the competition will breeze right past you. Have you become complacent? Have you stopped growing?

Take On New Challenges—Now is the Time

As a leader or a "wanna be" leader, know that now is the best time to enhance your skills. Volunteer to take on different responsibilities. Instead of pointing out problems, be the first to come up with solutions—and then spearhead their implementation. Roll up your sleeves and get uncomfortable!

In a challenging economy, leaders matter, and in today's tough times especially, they matter even more. Are you joining in the negative talk with your team members? Or even worse, are you leading the gloom-and-doom discussions? Stop all of the depressing water cooler chatter and encourage team members to get uncomfortable. Allow them opportunities to grow and stretch. Your business will be all the better for it.

Lead the way out of your comfort zone and into your *discomfort* zone to grow your skills, your value, and your organization's bottom line!

Leadership Lagniappe

To add more spice – tools and
techniques – for Getting Clear
on Your Assets, go to

http://www.ledetmanagement.com/freeresources

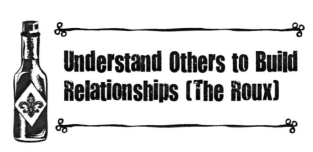

Understand Others to Build Relationships (The Roux)

Understand Others to Build Relationships
First, You Make a Roux

In South Louisiana, an old saying goes something like this: "If you want to cook a great meal, build a house, or fix a car, first you make a roux!"

This is especially true when it comes to making gumbo (the food) and GUMBO for effective leadership. Every Cajun makes his or her own special style of gumbo, yet one rule remains: *First, you make a roux!*

What is a roux? It's a thickening agent that forms the foundation for your gumbo. It essentially provides the building block for many Cajun dishes including jambalayas, étouffées, stews—and the list goes on.

How do you make a roux? Well, simply take a pot (preferably a big black cast iron pot) and put in equal parts oil and flour. Then cook this oil/flour combo on the stove, stirring continuously as it browns.

Now, although I say to use equal parts flour and oil, I (just like my Mimi—my grandmother—before me) never measure a thing. On the bayou where I'm from, most cooks don't need to measure or follow a recipe. That's because they put heart and soul into everything they cook. The point is, whether you take out your measuring cup or simply eyeball it, you want to patiently let your roux "develop" under a watchful eye. Stir it without stopping until it reaches a beautiful caramel color.

In the GUMBO leadership recipe, your first step is to take

stock of what you have on hand. That means going within and getting to know the assets—the ingredients—you have to work with. That's your foundation.

The second step in the GUMBO leadership recipe is knowing others—understanding who they are and the roles they play. Just as the roux builds the foundation for Cajun dishes, understanding people forms the basis not only for great leadership but for great sales, great teamwork, great service—and *this* list goes on.

But unless you're living on a desert island, guess what? You have to interact with other humanoids, look outward, and strive to understand the people around you.

So far in this GUMBO recipe, we've focused on your strengths, preferences, and behaviors. But unless you're living on a desert island, guess what? You have to interact with other humanoids, look outward, and strive to understand the people around you.

How to Tune In to Others

Developing the social awareness (understanding others) ingredient requires tuning in. How? By becoming highly observant and graciously reacting to people's *emotions*. Notice their body language, the words they use, their tone of voice. Listen to what they're saying—and what they're *not* saying. When interacting with them, always give your full attention.

In my workshops, I teach people a social awareness technique called People Reading. You can develop this skill by simply paying attention to the cues and clues that others constantly give you. When you do, you'll pick up on another person's style preferences and perspectives. Although you might find it tough being accurate with this People Reading skill at first, with practice you'll find it invaluable in both communicating and connecting with others.

For example, in South Louisiana, you'll often hear people greet each other with "Hey comment ca va?" ("How are you doing?") That question will often be followed by "How's ya Mama 'n' 'em?" (that is, your mother and the rest of the family).

Yes, Cajun life revolves around family and community. Cajuns enjoy taking time to listen to your concerns and helping out wherever possible.

Community "Roux" in Action

Having social awareness means being empathetic, service-minded, and generous—terms that definitely describe community-minded Cajuns. When Hurricane Katrina hit in August, 2005, those in Lafourche Parish (including my family and me) were mercifully spared much of the devastation. We experienced lots of wind damage and had no electrical power for a week, but our damage was nothing compared to what people in New Orleans suffered after the levees broke. (We actually didn't learn details about the devastation in New Orleans until days later. We had no TV coverage due to the power outage and, besides, we were incredibly busy helping evacuees.)

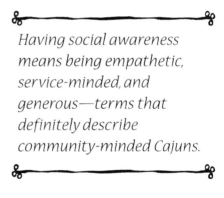

Having social awareness means being empathetic, service-minded, and generous—terms that definitely describe community-minded Cajuns.

In the day or two after the hurricane blew through, a shelter for special needs medical patients and their families was set up at our local university, Nicholls State University. Buses brought these patients and their families to be housed and cared for in the nursing building on campus.

Many evacuees came by bus to get a meal and dry clothes, which were especially needed by those who'd been plucked off the

Just as the roux provides the foundation for Cajun dishes, your ability to understand others, listen up, tune in, and reach out is the foundation for your leadership success.

roofs of their homes. The intention was to drive these evacuees to a shelter in Alexandria, Louisiana, about 185 miles away. Soon, however, word came that the Alexandria shelter was full, so the evacuees stayed on our campus.

When news about the shelter on campus spread, the community rallied in full force, bringing neighbors and churches together for a single purpose. Everyone cleaned out their freezers and did what we Cajuns do best—cooked and shared our bounty with the evacuees. We also cleaned out our closets and thrift stores, providing them with clothing, shoes, toiletries, and bedding. All this came together long before Red Cross representatives ever showed up!

This brand of compassion—putting ourselves in someone else's shoes—has been the "roux" of the people in South Louisiana forever. It mixes well with the recipe for great leadership, too!

Just as the roux provides the foundation for Cajun dishes, your ability to understand others, listen up, tune in, and reach out is the foundation for your leadership success.

Don't Burn the Roux!

In virtually any job, your success is influenced by your ability to understand, communicate with, and get along with other people. You interact with people whose positions are above you, below you, and on the same level as yours—not to mention customers, vendors, and suppliers. Especially in workplaces where teamwork is vital to performing effectively, you likely already stress strong people skills.

But if you fail at the crucial step of understanding and relating to others, your ability to lead is doomed. You burn the roux.

If you've been even half awake in your interactions with others, you've noticed that people approach projects, problems, and opportunities from different angles. Individuals have varying behavioral styles, diverse communication preferences, and special ways of seeing the same set of circumstances. As a leader, your ability to recognize and be sensitive to these variations can mean the difference between satisfying success and abject failure.

In cooking a gumbo—or any of the delectable Cajun dishes that begin with a roux—it's vitally important that you stir the roux continuously until it browns to the desired color. Be careful! If you answer the phone or get distracted for just a moment, your roux could burn. Once you have even one black speck in it, your whole house will smell of burnt roux and there's no salvaging it. Believe me, I speak from experience!

> *It's not only important to know the value of diverse perspectives within your team; you have to share your understanding with everyone in the circle.*

Yes, you can have all the best ingredients for your gumbo—fresh seafood or meats, vegetables, and seasonings—but if you fail at this one foundational step, your dish is doomed.

The same holds true in your leadership role. You can have all of the advanced degrees in the world, training up the wazoo (a highly technical term), and years of hands-on experience. But if you fail at the crucial step of understanding and relating to others, your ability to lead is doomed. You burn the roux.

What Causes Clashes?

When you bring together people with different personalities and behavioral styles, conflict is almost inevitable. Most clashes stem from a simple lack of understanding. If a co-worker does something you disagree with, it's easy to conclude he or she is uninformed, careless, or just plain wrong.

Chances are, you're failing to realize that "different" isn't wrong; it's just, well, *different*. Yet it's those differences that provide diverse perspectives and often result in creative solutions to problems.

Having a work group that gets along and communicates well requires awareness and understanding of others. A recent survey by *HR Executive* magazine found that the typical manager spends a full 18 percent of his or her time resolving conflicts among workers.[9] According to clients I work with, some spend even more time than that playing referee. It's not only important to know the value of diverse perspectives within your team; you have to share your understanding with everyone in the circle.

Unfortunately, many organizations invest a lot in technical training for their employees but little in the people skills that can have immense impact. Providing teambuilding retreats and interpersonal skills training is well worth the time and money. Why? Because improving interaction skills leads to enhanced teamwork, better communication, lower turnover, and ultimately, more effective customer service.

As a *lagniappe* (something extra) from that training, you'll find that employees enjoy expanded career success and promotional opportunities.

So in your leadership role, make sure to recognize, understand, and value the different styles and personalities on your team. And stay alert; don't burn the roux!

How's Ya Mama 'n' 'Em?

How's Ya Mama 'n' 'Em?

No, I haven't taken leave of my grammatical senses. This common expression in South Louisiana is our way of asking how a person is doing, how their family is doing, and what's going on in their lives outside of work. And it's a huge practice in our culture—one that, when used in all interactions with others, could change your work culture, too.

Taking a few minutes to engage others in talking about themselves reflects an investment in the relationship. Most people feel flattered that you care enough to ask. The key, though, is that your interest must be sincere and genuine, not like your interactions with your "pseudo friends" on Facebook (or as my friend James calls it, Spacebook).

Theodore Roosevelt is credited as saying, "People don't care how much you know until they know how much you care." This holds true for your team members as well as your customers. In fact, in many ways, you should treat your employees as you would a valued customer. And yes, it does take effort and time. But consider it a deposit in your relationship "account" and strive to make more deposits than you do withdrawals in that account.

Who's *Not* in the Relationship Business?

In a chat with a client recently, she said, "Well, you know, we're really in the relationship business." As I noodled that, my first thought was, "Well, show me an organization that's *not* in the relationship business."

Let's face it. If you're in business at all—regardless of the industry or product or service you provide—you're in the relationship business.

And people do business with people they know, like, and trust.

Similarly, team members become loyal, committed, and engaged when their leader is someone they know, like, and trust.

Relationships—building, nurturing, and maintaining them—form the core of your business. Without customers, you'd have no reason for being. Without employees, you couldn't provide the goods or services to your customers—or at least not in a timely fashion.

A Skill That's Learned

This ability to take an interest in others may not come naturally for everyone. And that's okay, because it's a skill you can learn. One introverted client asked for coaching in this area. He was so analytical by nature, he wanted a specific formula for creating great relationships. He even asked me how many minutes he would need to engage in a personal conversation with team members. (I could picture him setting an egg timer to time it precisely!)

Sorry, there is no magic formula for creating great relationships, but do experiment with these Cajun tips:

- Ask questions about the other person's family. (You can start with "How's ya Mama 'n' 'em?")

- Notice what he or she talks about casually (like hobbies, grandchildren, etc.) and ask about these interests. ("How long have you been carving duck decoys?")

- Make a mental note of, say, the person's weekend plans so on Monday morning, you can ask how the activity went. ("How was the fishing/crabbing trip? Did ya'll catch anything? I must've missed your call inviting me to your fish fry/crab boil.")

- Engage in brief group conversations after a big weekend event. ("How 'bout dem Saints?")

Know that your ability to influence team members to perform and produce hinges directly on the relationships you have created with them. Consider taking an interest in them and their families and life outside of work a small investment that has potentially huge returns.

What? You say you can't afford to take the time to converse with employees and customers? I say you can't afford *not* to. Your business success depends on it.

By the way, "How's ya Mama 'n' 'em?"

Gumbo Ya Ya

If you've ever spent time in bayou country, you know that Cajuns love to talk. And depending on their passion for their subject, they can gesture wildly as they speak. It doesn't matter where they are—a family gathering, a church function, a PTA event, a business meeting, or even a wake or a funeral—Cajuns get animated when they talk and don't care who else is speaking at the same time.

In South Louisiana, the expression *gumbo ya ya* actually has nothing to do with gumbo or any kind of food. Rather, it describes a scene in which everyone wildly chatters at once. This occurs frequently in Cajun culture; does it happen in your organization, too? Do you participate in any of the *gumbo ya ya* that goes on among your team members? Or do you take time to listen to their concerns in a meaningful way?

As a leader, you might be so busy barking out directions, assigning tasks, and giving instructions, you don't think about taking time to hear what others are telling you. But by becoming a better listener, you'll increase your own productivity as well as that of your team. You'll improve your ability to influence, persuade, and delegate. What's more, you'll avoid conflict and misunderstandings on the road to resolving problems with customers, co-workers, and bosses—all necessary for workplace success.

Be a Good Listener

Clearly, success stems from listening well, a skill you likely use more than any other kind. To consciously practice your listening skills, follow these do's and don'ts—guidelines you'll find handy in all locales and relationships:

- *Do* ask for and really listen to what others say. You may be surprised at the insight they offer.

- *Don't* interrupt, draw conclusions, or judge the speaker.

- *Do* open your ears, mind, and heart to the suggestions of others, to new ideas, and to creative solutions.

- *Don't* assume you already know what others are about to say, or worse, finish their sentences for them.

- *Do* listen to what's being said as well as what's *not* being said. Often team members have insight into a problem but need to feel safe from judgment or condemnation before opening up. As a leader, what you don't know *can* hurt you!

- *Don't* focus on your next statement while the other person's speaking. Waiting for your turn to say something is *not* listening!

- *Do* maintain eye contact with those who are speaking, giving them your full attention. Have you ever tried to talk about something important to someone who was multitasking? It's frustrating! So when others attempt to talk to you, give them the respect of being fully present and attentive.

Continually work on achieving good listening skills for yourself and model them for your team members. Don't let *gumbo ya ya* become part of *your* organization's culture!

Don't Put Strychnine in My Gumbo!

"**I** don't care who you are or what your title is; if I don't trust you, I can't work with you!" Louis said vehemently.

We were in a leadership development workshop discussing the integral role that trust plays, particularly among a manager and his or her team members. Louis serves as a lead operator on an oil rig in the Gulf of Mexico. His rationale behind the statement he made isn't hard to understand. In his role, he puts life and limb on the line every day, and if he can't be absolutely sure his co-workers are acting safely and not cutting corners, he doesn't want to work with them.

Whether you're a leader by title or by influence, trust is an integral part of leadership in a work relationship and any other kind of relationship.

You may not tackle life-and-death situations in your workplace, but I can assure you, trust is just as important for you as it is for Louis. Whether you're a leader by title or by influence, trust is an integral part of leadership in a work relationship and any other kind of relationship.

If I'm only trustworthy in *some* ways but not *all* ways, it's like adding strychnine to a huge pot of gumbo and saying only part of the gumbo is poisoned. (Give me a shot or two of Tabasco in my gumbo, but I'll pass on the poison!)

As author Cheryl Biehl says, "One of the realities of life is that if you can't trust a person at all points, you can't truly trust him at any point." Are you earning your team members' trust by acting consistently?

Showing Confidence

Consistent behavior goes both ways. If you trust in others, you will be trusted in return. Here's an example. When I was just starting my career, I worked with a manager who assigned me an important project and let me run with it. Nothing could have been more motivating or inspiring than knowing she had confidence in me. I wanted to do a great job to show her she'd made the right judgment call.

> *If you let your team members know you believe in them, they'll strive to produce positive results. They'll even run through brick walls for you to not let you down.*

If you let your team members know you believe in them, they'll strive to produce positive results. They'll even run through brick walls for you to not let you down.

Think about someone who made a significant difference in your life—a boss, a coach, a teacher, even a parent or grandparent. How did it feel when they expressed their confidence in your abilities and showed complete trust in you? I'm sure you remember.

Don't put strychnine in your relationship gumbo—ever! Show your team members you believe in them—and keep making deposits in their trust accounts.

Tete á Tete Communication

I'm dating myself, I know, but I can still remember when we got long-distance calls from a relative or friend out of state. The operator came on and said, "I have a person-to-person call for so-and-so." I never quite understood how that worked, but I guess long distance calls cost so much, the people calling didn't want to waste precious minutes and money talking to someone else first!

Yet in the process of making progress, what's been lost? You guessed it. One-on-one communication with others.

This sped-up world offers more and better technology, cool gadgets, and time-saving gizmos. Yet 24/7 electronic access doesn't guarantee real *connections with* other human beings.

Here on the bayou, I've often heard the term *tête á tête*. When Mama said to me, "We need to have a *tête á tête!*" she wanted to have a talk with me head to head and eyeball to eyeball. It also meant I was likely in some kind of trouble. (I seem to remember a lot of those *tête á têtes*, and that's because I was always causing some kind of *misère* in one way or another!) In a business setting, though, it would simply involve having a one-on-one conversation with someone, an in-person meeting.

Do you email the guy in the cubicle next to you rather than walk over and have a *tête á tête*? Do you text message your friend to see how she's doing after a serious family problem instead of giving her a call or dropping by to visit?

Now, I'm not saying that texting and emailing are always inappropriate or that you should never use them. I believe, though, that as a leader, you'll realize a huge amount of value when you connect with your team members in person. Call a meeting when you need to or walk over and meet in person!

Don't Blame the Meeting Itself

Sure, I know you're saying something like this: "But most meetings completely waste my time. I'm suffering from an agonizing condition known as death-by-meeting!" More often than not, it's because the leader and/ or attendees failed to properly prepare, or include the right people, or keep the meeting focused and productive. Don't blame the meeting itself!

Yes, using email often seems more expedient and efficient, but not if you consider the cost of what you're missing by not conducting an in-person meeting.

But when you have intentional person-to-person meetings, you can see your fellow team member roll his eyes at your new procedures, or cross her arms in frustration, or nod his head in agreement. It's invaluable in helping you "hear" what's not being said! Yes, using email often seems more expedient and efficient, but not if you consider the cost of what you're missing by *not* conducting an in-person meeting.

When you take into account that your tone of voice and body language are completely removed from your written message, you leave a lot of room for interpretation (or misinterpretation), assumptions, and misunderstanding.

Choose the Best Medium for Connecting

As a leader, when communicating important information to team members, think carefully about the medium you use. If you want to get honest feedback, express concerns, or give performance feedback, your objectives are best served if you meet *tête á tête*. *Connect with* others rather than talk *at* them.

I heard a manager talking about one of his team members this way: "I sent him a text and I TOLD him to . . . ." And I'm sure he did tell his team member what he wanted done. But did he give the person a chance to ask questions or paraphrase back to the manager his directions? Did the manager actually demonstrate what he wanted done? I doubt it.

In a cryptic text message riddled with abbreviations and code words, you can't know if the recipient understood your message or whether your code was misconstrued.

HTH! CWYL mayB F2F! Translation: *Hope that helps! Chat with you later maybe face to face!*

> *Connect with others rather than talk at them.*

Never underestimate the power and value of sitting down eyeball to eyeball—*tête á tête*—with your team members for a person-to-person convo. You'll be surprised what you hear that's *not* being said.

Listen with Your Eyes

Little Marie, a Cajun girl from down the bayou, came home from school excited about the drawing she had created in art class. She skipped into the kitchen, practically bursting at the seams with excitement.

"Mama, Mama, guess what?" she asked.

Her mother, focused on preparing supper, said, "*Mae cher,* what you makin' all the *roogaroo for?*"

"Guess what?" the little girl squealed.

"What?" the mama asked, not looking up from the *roux* she was browning.

"Mama, you're not listenin'!"

"*Mae cher,* I am too listenin'!"

"But Mama," the little girl pleaded, "you're not listenin' with your *eyes.*"

I love this story because it points out the importance of active listening. As a leader, you probably communicate a lot during the course of your day. One of the most important skills you can develop is your ability to listen effectively.

Like little Marie said, sometimes you need to listen with your *eyes.* Pay attention to body language. Make eye contact. Focus on what's not being said.

Reading Between the Lines

A great leader reads between the lines and hears what's *not* being said as well as what is. (Of course, the same holds true for great sales representatives, team members, customer service agents, parents, spouses, and so on.)

While your tongue conveys information verbally, your body talks, too. Indeed, anytime you speak to someone, your body makes a statement. When a team member comes to you to ask a question, do you impatiently tap your fingers on your desk, glance over at your inbox, even cross your arms and set your jaw? That's your body talking.

> *Notice I said **connect**—not necessarily **communicate**—with each person. After all, isn't the purpose of communicating with others to **connect** with them?*

Communication goes the other way, too. People constantly give cues and clues about their preferences, personalities, and meanings. Successful leaders learn to pick up on these signals and use them to better connect with each person.

Notice I said *connect*—not necessarily *communicate*—with each person. After all, isn't the purpose of communicating with others to *connect* with them?

Where's the Attention Going?

You've probably had this happen to you: You want to tell someone—maybe your spouse or boss or co-worker—about something that happened to you. However, that person is reading the newspaper, typing an email or text message, or just reorganizing the contents of a drawer. Clearly, you're not being listened to. Even if he or she could repeat verbatim what you just said, you still feel like that person's activity got more attention than you and your issue did.

In the work environment, nothing extinguishes an employee's enthusiasm faster than a leader who doesn't listen. So when a team member comes to you with a concern, stop, look him or her in the eye, and focus on the words being spoken. If you're involved in something else, ask to schedule a time to talk when you can give your full attention (and I don't mean two weeks from Tuesday!).

Focus on What's Being Said

By focusing on what's being said, looking that person in the eye, and asking questions, you demonstrate your respect and interest. As you do, seek to pick up on nuances that aren't being articulated. That's part of listening, too.

In the work environment, nothing extinguishes an employee's enthusiasm faster than a leader who doesn't listen.

In the world of email, texting, and instant messaging, communication can get lost when people can't see the postures, gestures, or facial expressions of others. Now, I'm not saying never text or email (I'm as guilty as the next gal!). But when you're conveying important information with team members, think carefully about the best medium to use for the situation.

Remember, to gain effectiveness and credibility as a leader, nothing replaces listenin' with your eyes.

Get Back to Basics

Growing up in the Cajun culture, I'm ashamed to admit that I often take much for granted. It has taken me years to fully appreciate the abundant way of life we enjoy, but I'm so happy and proud to now pass this culture down to my children.

Since before I can remember, my parents had a "camp" at Grand Isle. While Louisiana has lots of coastline, we have only one beach and that's Grand Isle. Our family spent every summer weekend on the island, two full weeks during the summer, and as many weekends as my parents could squeeze in during the school year. Spending that much time down there, Mama and Daddy used to say we were living "off the water" instead of living off the land. We fished, crabbed, and trawled for our meals. Then we enjoyed bountiful, delectable crab and shrimp boils, fish, shrimp, and oyster fries, and an abundance of good food. Mmmm! *Ca c'est bon!*

We always had lots of family around—my brothers and sisters and their families, aunts, uncles, and lots of cousins. We played cards, told stories, water skied, and enjoyed the beach together.

Looking back, I realize I learned a lot in those experiences. Mostly, I learned the basics of how to treat people and the important things in life.

There are *beaucoup* management and leadership theories available these days—so many that they rival the number of snowball flavors at Jeaux's Snowball Stand! (Snowballs are shaved ice drenched in sweet syrup, and they're available during the summer in South Louisiana.)

But why complicate things? Like our family did at Grand Isle, let's go back to the basics.

Simple Principles of Living

Decades ago, Robert Fulghum wrote *All I Really Need to Know I Learned in Kindergarten*.[10] Recently, I pulled it off the bookshelf and thumbed through its pages to remind me how true his principles remain today—and how they apply to leadership as well as to children.

> *Let your mind review those "play fair" rules posted above the blackboard in school and recall that everyone is human just as you are.*

Read in a fresh way, this book reminds all leaders (myself included) to get back to basics. That means inspiring, engaging, and influencing others to achieve results. The most effective leaders actually do so using the same simple rules children are taught in kindergarten.

I highlight three of Fulghum's principles here.

Play fair. You'd think this goes without saying, but it's easy to get caught up in the "busyness" of life and forget to live by the Golden Rule or neglect to do what you said you'd do. Perhaps you don't give others the benefit of the doubt or you engage in unkind gossip. Maybe you even point the finger of blame and lose your cool.

As a leader, it can be tough to be even-handed and to do the right thing. But pause to reflect and go back to the basics as often as possible. Let your mind review those "play fair" rules posted above the blackboard in school and recall that everyone is human just as you are. After all, a leadership title doesn't *entitle* anyone to abuse or disrespect others. In fact, as a leader, you're expected to model fairness just as your kindergarten teacher taught it to you.

Say you're sorry when you hurt someone. Why can this be so difficult? Some leaders fear that if they fess up to their failures, faults, or frailties, they'll appear vulnerable and risk losing the respect of their team members. *Au contraire.* Admitting you made a mistake that hurt someone, apologizing sincerely, and vowing to make it right will build trust and loyalty among the members of your team.

When you go out into the world, watch out for traffic, hold hands, and stick together. Isn't this just a simplified description of teamwork? If you've been in highly competitive work environments, you might have learned that "in order for me to win, someone else has to lose." However, in today's strained economy, companies realize the value of teaming up to create greater employee engagement and encourage creativity and innovation.

Regardless of your title, your ultimate job is to help your organization achieve bottom-line results by building a team spirit at work. What happens when you look out for each other? You create a cul-

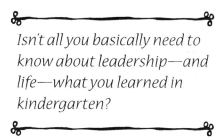

Isn't all you basically need to know about leadership—and life—what you learned in kindergarten?

ture of cooperation and collaboration. By sticking together, you'll achieve your common goals—and enjoy a win/win way of working and living.

Clearly, by not coming up with a profound new management theory or philosophical leadership approach, I've taken the easy way out. Still, I think it's silly to reinvent the wheel. Isn't all you basically need to know about leadership—and life—what you learned in kindergarten?

Now, if you'll excuse me, it's time for my afternoon nap. Yours, too.

It's Not About You

I know that this belief—that it's not about you—might come as a shock. But it's true. It's about them. In fact, it's *always been about them*. Life is about *connecting with* other people.

One of the greatest qualities you can develop as a leader—or a team member, a friend, a spouse—is humility. *Merriam-Webster* defines *humility* as the quality of being modest, respectful, or humble. *Humble* is defined as modest and unassuming in attitude and behavior; feeling or showing respect and deference toward other people; not proud or haughty; not arrogant or assertive.

Does this sound wimpy or weak to you? *Au contraire, mon amie!*

People who are humble—or as we say in my neck of the woods, *il est mortifier*—actually have immense inner strength. They feel so secure and confident in their own abilities, they don't need constant approval or a desire to bask in the limelight. And they certainly don't need to *vanter*, or brag, about their accomplishments.

Ways to Boost Your Humility

How can you boost your leadership effectiveness by becoming more humble as you interact with others? Practice these four ways:

- **Be sincerely more interested in the other person than you are in yourself.** Ask questions and listen to his or her answers about what's going on. If you're not sincere—well, people can spot a phony baloney a mile away. Faking interest in someone else so you can get something *you* want borders on manipulation. That's definitely *not* what humility is all about.

- **Let the other person shine and be the star of the situation.** It's never about you and your accomplishments. Rather, your job is to draw out the best that others have to give, not to put into them what you think was left out. Draw out the greatness in others at work. Set up your people for success and then step out of their way so they can shine.

- **Admit you don't know everything.** This might be more difficult than apologizing or admitting you've made a mistake. But allow someone else to have the last answer. Be open to learning from everyone, regardless of the title or authority a person might have.

- **Look for ways *to* serve others.** Listen, *really* listen, to what people say. Note their interests, concerns, and anything else you hear about them. Keep your ears open for ways you can help them or connect them to someone else who can fill a need.

I recently met someone at a professional association meeting and enjoyed chatting with him for several minutes. By the time we parted, I knew his name, where he lives, his educational background, what he does professionally, where he met his wife, and how long they'd been married! Two months later, he was the featured speaker at another association meeting. In fact, he was the reason I attended the meeting. There, he addressed the importance of *humility* and *authenticity* in leadership. Later, he asked a colleague my name and wondered aloud if we'd met before. Sadly, he had no memory of our earlier conversation—even the one we'd had that day! Why? Because it had been all about *him*. He didn't ask questions about my life nor (apparently) did he give a hoot about me.

By the way, his presentation *a` l'échec ou de flop* – or went over like a lead balloon. Like I said, people can spot a phony baloney a mile away.

When you forget yourself and focus on lifting up and developing others, you show what humility means in everyday life.

Leadership Lagniappe

To expand your seasoning options –
get more resources – to help you
Understand Others, go to

http://www.ledetmanagement.com/freeresources

Modify Your Approach to Season the Conversation
("The Cajun Four Seasons")

-The Cajun Four Seasons

Back to our gumbo recipe . . . .

If you've watched the roux carefully and haven't let it burn, what's the next step?

Cajun cooking has become known to the rest of the world as super-spicy to the point of being almost inedible. I've seen demonstrations that include coating the food with cayenne pepper and then dousing it with hot sauce—and they crazily call this "Cajun". What a misrepresentation of our delectable dishes!

Cajun cooking, like the entire Cajun culture, is what I would call "flavorful" because we Cajuns add our uniqueness to everything we do—from cooking to art to music. We season them all with heart and soul. It's a way of life for us.

In authentic Cajun cooking, almost every dish begins with what's referred to as The Trinity—onions, celery, and bell pepper—three basic vegetables that add delicious flavor without overpowering the dish. Garlic is always a key ingredient as well, so we can't leave it out. We put garlic on just about everything except our breakfast cereal!

So these four veggies form the foundation for many Cajun dishes. In fact, I've heard it said that when asked to name the four seasons, a Cajun will respond "Onions, bell pepper, celery, and garlic" instead of "winter, spring, summer, and fall."

When you throw the "Cajun Four Seasons" into a roux that's

been browned "just so," they give off an aroma like no other that smells delicious as the roux smothers down in the pot. *Cher de Mon Dieu! Talk about smells good!* It makes everyone within smelling distance want to check out what's cooking.

Each of the Four Seasons contributes its essence to give the gumbo a rich depth of flavor that can't be replaced. I'd never even think about leaving out any one of these basics!

Your Leadership GUMBO

In a successful leadership recipe, each team member adds a unique flavor to the team, thus, requiring a different approach with each individual. Just as each of the Cajun Four Seasons contributes to our gumbo's rich flavor, team members contribute their unique personalities, strengths, skills, and roles to create an effective work team – a GUMBO that's great.

A well-seasoned mixture of styles results in—

- creativity,

- innovation,

- diverse perspectives, and

- outstanding service.

Ah! *Ca c'est bon!* (That's good!)

But with a diverse team comes opportunities for miscommunications, disconnects, and misunderstandings. Do those problems ever arise in your team? They usually happen when you think you've communicated clearly what you wanted and apparently the other person heard something else. Why? This is usually due to the fact that we have different communication styles, perspectives, and filters through which all of our interactions pass. It's as though people speak different languages based on their communication style. But through understanding and practice, you *can* learn to "speak their language."

Speaking Cajun French

English was a second language for many people born and raised along the bayous and in the prairies and swamps of South Louisiana. Often they spoke nothing but Cajun French at home and started learning English when they went to school. Cajun French originates from the language spoken by the French and Acadian people who settled in Louisiana after being booted out of Acadia in the 17th century. The French that the Cajuns speak is actually a mélange of Parisian French and fractured English and varies in pronunciation, meaning, and spelling, depending on what area you're from. Sadly, in an effort to force children to learn English and forsake their Cajun upbringing, teachers once punished young children for speaking Cajun French with a sharp rap from a ruler on their wrists or knuckles.

It's as though people speak different languages based on their communication style. But through understanding and practice, you can learn to "speak their language."

Despite these efforts to squelch the language, many do still speak Cajun French, and some folks, especially old-timers, actually feel more comfortable speaking French. Those who greet them speaking French exemplify the skill of modifying their approach to make that valued personal connection.

Because members of younger generations in Louisiana don't hear Cajun French as much as their parents or their *mamans* and *papas* (grandparents) did, most of them can't speak the language. In Mama's case, Mimi and Papa (my grandparents) wanted to converse with each other without the children knowing what they were saying. So they used Cajun French as a secret language. It worked! Mama said their conversations always went right over her head.

Make Meaningful Connections

While you may not communicate in a foreign language, you still want to tune into the other person's interest. If you don't, your communication with him or her could fall on deaf ears.

If you don't pay attention to the person's way of communicating, you can totally blow making a connection. But if you take your message and translate it into that person's language, your message will likely be received as you intended it.

Here's what I know: If you don't pay attention to the person's way of communicating, you can totally blow making a connection. But if you take your message and translate it into that person's language, your message will likely be received as you intended it. The solution? Modify your approach with everyone to enjoy a meaningful connection.

Pause a moment and think about the best leader you've ever known. What made that person special? Was your connection based on his or her actions, characteristics, or attitude toward you? I'm willing to bet that person long ago mastered tailoring communication with you so that instead of just communicating he was really connecting and engaging with you.

Any one-size-fits-all approach just doesn't cut it.

Just as the Cajun Four Seasons contribute flavorful tastes to your gumbo, so do a diverse mixture of personalities, strengths, styles, and skills add to your working environment. As a leader, leveraging the rich diversity of your teams requires modifying your approach with each individual, speaking that person's language, and connecting in a meaningful way.

What flavors can you add to spice up your relationships?

Boudreaux and Thibodaux

"Boudreaux" and "Thibodaux" are the lovable, laughable central characters in much of South Louisiana humor. In fact, they're essential players in many Cajun jokes. We love to laugh at their flat Cajun accents and their often dim-witted antics.

They could only happen in South Louisiana—or could they?

While the subject matter is perhaps universal, the characters give it a unique flavor.

(Please know that Boudreaux and Thibodaux are also common family names in Louisiana. The antics of these two characters in no way reflect on members of these fine families.)

So on with my story about their antics . . . .

Reverend Boudreaux was the pastor of the local Cajun Baptist Church and Father Thibodaux was the priest of the St. Pius Catholic Church across the road. They were both standing by the road pounding into the ground a sign that read:

Da End is Near

Turn Yo Sef 'Roun Now

Afore It's Too Late!

As a car sped past them, the driver leaned out his window and yelled, "You religious nuts!" From the proximity of the curve in the road, they hear screeching tires and then a big splash. That's when the Reverend Boudreaux turned to Father Thibodaux and asked, "Do ya tink maybe da sign should jus say 'Bridge Out'?"

Communication Casser

While we can laugh at Boudreaux and Thibodaux, can you see yourself in their blunders? How many times have you communicated something in a way you thought was clear and straightforward, only to get completely different results than you wanted or expected?

Communication breakdowns—in this case, communication crashes—happen all the time and can cost time, effort, productivity, and lost opportunities. In South Louisiana when something is broken, we say it is *casser.* (Of course, we also use the same term to refer to someone who's had too much to drink, but that's another story.)

Don't let *your* communication become *casser.* Because your ability to connect with others directly affects bottom-line results, having clear communication skills are key to your effectiveness as a leader.

Be sure to keep the following guidelines in mind.

Over-do it. Many leaders falsely believe they communicate *enough.* But in my experience, you can't communicate with your team *too much.* Strong leaders err on the side of *over*-communication to ensure that their messages have been received.

Get "in sync." Follow these directions:

Take your right hand and touch your right ear.

Take your left hand and touch your nose.

Tap your right toe three times.

Pat your left knee with your left hand.

Were you able to follow these instructions? Participants in my workshops comply with them without a problem. Why? Because they understand exactly what I mean when I say right hand, right ear, and so on. You must admit, these directions are simple and explicit—like you should be.

Define your terms. Why do most miscommunications happen in the workplace and on the job? Because commonly defined terms and standards are rarely simple and explicit. For example, can you spell out good definitions of the following terms?

- good communication skills

- excellent customer service

- punctuality

- a good worker

- a job well done

I'll bet your definitions differ from mine, and mine differ from the next guy's. That's why, when coaching employees, be sure to take pains to convey—explicitly and up front—all the expectations you have for your team members. Don't assume they know and agree with your definitions of these terms. Often, managers become frustrated because one of their team members isn't doing a "good job." In fact, they never sat down with that individual and explained what a "good job" meant! Always get "in sync" on your definitions of the terms you use.

> *That's why, when coaching employees, be sure to take pains to convey—explicitly and up front—all the expectations you have for your team members.*

Ask to repeat the instructions. It might seem like a waste of time at first, but it's a good idea to ask your listeners to tell you, in their own words, what they'll do as a result of your conversation. More often than not, having them paraphrase your directions will illuminate—and eliminate—areas of miscommunication or misunderstanding.

Bear the burden and blame. After giving directions or making a request of a team member, if you ask, "Do you have any questions?" or "Do you understand?" You will rarely uncover any miscommunications. Instead ask, "What part have I failed to make clear?" This way, you're not implying "What part of my message are you too stupid to get?" (which I *know* you're never thinking). Instead, you're implying that if a communication breakdown took place, it happened on your end, not theirs.

Be picky. Yes, Boudreaux and Thibodaux could have been more effective had they chosen a different medium or wording for their message. You, too, need to be picky about the medium you use. Obviously, if your message is an urgent life-or-death warning, choose the medium that can deliver it as quickly and efficiently as possible.

Meet in person. Ideally, most of a manager's communication time is spent—face to face—with direct reports in order to provide immediate feedback. Consider this the richest information medium of all. Why? Because you can observe voice, eye contact, posture, and body language. When do you meet in person? When you're delegating, coaching, disciplining, answering questions, and building rapport.

Use the phone. Communicating by telephone is appropriate for quick exchanges of information and monitoring progress. I especially appreciate that it saves travel time, but it's not appropriate for everything—such as discussing disciplinary matters.

Use email or texting. With any kind of written communication, you lose the vocal and visual part of the message. Written words can be interpreted differently than intended—just ask Boudreaux and Thibodaux.

Your job? Learn from their communication *casser* and consciously communicate with others clearly every time.

Autre Pays, Autre Coutume . . .

Autre pays, autre coutume, or as ya'll might say, "When in Rome, do as the Romans do."

For the past three years, my daughter traveled to Europe and, when in Rome, she did as the Romans do—she spoke Italian. Or as Ricky Bobby (Will Ferrell) from the movie *Talladega Nights* would say, "We're in America and we speak American." Same concept.

You may have seen the video of twin baby boys in diapers carrying on a hilarious "conversation." If you haven't seen it, go to YouTube.com and type in Talking Twin Babies. I'm amazed at how they seem to speak *their* secret language. They really do "get" each other.

This adorable video reminds me of the importance of being sensitive to the other person's language. But how do you know what that is?

Watch for Clues and Cues

Each person constantly gives you cues and clues about his or her preferred communication style. It's up to you to watch and listen so you can figure out the other person's preferences, and then "translate" your message using a language or style that person can understand.

Now, I'm not suggesting you have to change your goals, expectations, or intended results. Rather, if you want others to really "get" you, speak *their* language.

> *Successful leaders—as well as successful sales professionals, service representatives, and team members—know that by using the same approach with each individual, they'd be effective only a small percentage of the time.*

I'm not a particular fan of text messaging (perhaps because my brain goes faster than my fingers can type on those little buttons). But I know my kids respond best to text messages. So when I want to tell them something quickly, I text them—*their* preferred way of communicating. Obviously, texting won't replace face-to-face, eyeball-to-eyeball, or *tête á tête* conversations, but to get their fastest response, I know it's the best method. (What's the "lagniappe" of using their preferred communication method? They often text me short thoughtful messages, wishing me luck for a speaking engagement or telling me thanks for all I do for them.)

More Clues and Cues

Successful leaders know the employees on their teams have different communication styles and motivational needs. Successful leaders—as well as successful sales professionals, service representatives, and team members—know that by using the same approach with each individual, they'd be effective only a small percentage of the time. Rather, they're adept at picking up on subtle cues and clues others give, and they adapt accordingly. Same message presented differently to each individual. For example:

Pay attention to how the other person communicates and mimic his or her style. Notice if the other person prefers communication to be:

- short, sweet, and to the point,

- casual, friendly, and enthusiastic,

- thoughtful, methodical, and sincere, or

- detailed, accurate, and factual.

No, the twins in the video aren't in Rome, but they definitely speak a foreign language. Most important, they're both fluent in the same language and truly connect with each other.

As a leader, are you truly connecting with your team members? Are you speaking *their* language?

The Raconteur's Gift

Every culture tells stories as a means of preserving its way of life. In South Louisiana, the *raconteurs,* or storytellers, pass along our history, culture, and perspective to the next generations. Cajuns love to sit on the porch swing, gather around campfires, and hear stories of Cajun lore passed down through multiple generations.

Of course, storytelling goes way back. Native Americans taught lessons through stories and so did Jesus in the Christian Bible. Cajun raconteurs passed on the history of the Acadians and their exile from eastern Canada and the story of their arrival in this new land with its strange wildlife and plants. They told how their people survived by adapting old customs and creating new ones.

Storytelling—probably the oldest form of communication— can become one of the best tools you could ever apply to your leadership goals. Yep, that's right. Storytelling can be a powerful leadership tool.

But, you might argue, business communication must be logical, linear, and objective, right? Not so. If you want to inspire, engage, and influence others (and what leader doesn't?), aim to stir their emotions and spark a desire to take action.

What Makes Storytelling Successful?

Good storytelling can make your message relevant, visual, memorable, interesting, and compelling. Let me explain how these elements contribute to your storytelling success.

Relevant. Facts, figures, and statistics have no intrinsic meaning unless they're tied to a story that gives them relevance. The late Steve Jobs brilliantly put technical information into terms and pictures everyone could relate to. When introducing new products, Jobs never spouted facts about the features of Apple's latest creation; he gave the product context and relevance to everyday living.

For instance, when introducing the iPod, instead of saying it had 30 GB of storage, he said it had enough memory for 7,500 songs, 25,000 pictures, or up to 75 hours of video. Now that "story" gave his message relevance to every consumer and potential Apple customer!

If you want to inspire, engage, and influence others (and what leader doesn't?), aim to stir their emotions and spark a desire to take action.

For your message to pack a powerful punch, don't only impart facts and data; provide information within a framework of context and perspective. That's what gives it meaning and relevance for your team members.

Visual. From the time my children were young, I read aloud to them every night. Naturally, they could listen better than they could read, so we quickly advanced from picture books to what we called "chapter" books. That's when my daughter was in kindergarten and my boys were still preschool age.

With no pictures to follow, I encouraged them to "paint a picture in their minds" of the story as I read it. The same principle applies for leaders, too. Your message will be more engaging if you evoke images and pictures in the minds of your listeners.

For instance, if you were to say that Louisiana loses 25 square miles of precious wetlands every year, it's not as visual as if you said we're losing our coastal wetlands at a rate of one football-field-sized area every 30 minutes.

When people can visualize what you're talking about, they can process the information more easily. Storytelling paints a verbal picture for your listeners.

Memorable. Policies and procedures may be necessary for you to have on paper, but if you want people to actually follow a certain protocol, tell them a story. Sadly, many HR folks are in the business of CYA—Cover Your Ass (sorry, I said many – not all) —and not focused on protecting their workforce.

For instance, if you want people to follow safety procedures, don't put out a written policy stating they have to wear a hardhat or seat belt. Instead, at your safety meeting, show photos of your children and the families of other team members. Stress that getting home to family is the reason for working safely. Touch their emotions. Tap into their internal motivations. When you tell stories that make your message memorable, they won't forget to wear their hardhats or buckle up.

Interesting. People love listening to a good story. They enjoy hearing the "before" part of the story, the struggle, and then the "after" or resolution of the struggle. And I'm not just talking about fiction stories, either.

One of the best storytellers ever is filmmaker Ken Burns, the director and producer of many award-winning documentaries on Public Broadcasting System (PBS). Burns has a remarkable way of taking historical events and weaving together a story in such an interesting way that a boring subject becomes absolutely riveting.

Another storytelling great was legendary radio commentator Paul Harvey. Nobody could turn to another station until they heard Harvey's "The Rest of the Story." I also had a History professor in college who was a brilliant storyteller and he had us sitting on the edge of our seats in every class.

So how can you impart information to get its importance across in an interesting way? Turn it into a story.

Compelling. Conveying information to your team (or cus-

Telling a story gives you a powerful medium for conveying your message— and will always inspire more action than delivering plain facts, data, or statistics ever could.

tomers or any other stakeholders) is necessary because you want to compel them to take action. For instance, if I tell you about the starving children in Africa, you may feel compassion or empathy, but you may not feel compelled to send money. However, if I show you photos of those same starving children, you may be so moved you pull out your checkbook to make a donation.

It's not enough to *tell* people to take action; you've got to *persuade* them through emotion. When you learn and practice ways to make your message compelling, your desired actions will follow.

What About Being Objective and Factual?

I know this concept of telling stories at work seems counterintuitive, especially if you've always believed business communications must be objective, factual, and—well—dry.

Yet as a leader, if you want to influence others, you're miles ahead if you adapt your approach to the situation and the people involved. Telling a story gives you a powerful medium for conveying your message—and will always inspire more action than delivering plain facts, data, or statistics ever could.

No, you don't need a porch swing to become the *raconteur* of your organization. Simply determine how to weave your message into a story that will move your team members.

Some Like it Hot!

Our Cajun food is known for having a rich depth of flavor, but people have their own preferences about how hot it should be.

No matter what I'm cooking or who's eating, I err on the "lite" side when it comes to spices. Then I place the Tabasco, Louisiana Hot Sauce, and Tony Chachere's Creole Seasoning Blend on the table so my guests can "heat" up their food to their liking.

As my mama often said, *chacque á son gout*, or to each his own.

The same approach works well when it comes to recognizing employees in the workplace. Did you know that recognition can be the greatest motivator for affecting the performance of all types of people?

> *Did you know that recognition can be the greatest motivator for affecting the performance of all types of people?*

As a leader, if you're serious about performance, you *have* to be serious about recognition. (And what leader or manager isn't serious about performance these days?) But to be effective, understand that people have their preferences. What works with one person may have the opposite effect with another. This isn't another management fad *du jour*; it's a tried-and-true principle—one that's needed to lead teams to greater performance.

Offer Positive Consequences

One of the most powerful ways to boost employee performance is to offer positive consequences for that performance. (This also works with children, spouses, and pets, by the way.) Although this may seem like common sense, it's surprising how few managers "get" it.

Before you shake your head and declare your tight budget won't allow any *hoity toity* (fancy schmancy) employee recognition program, hold on! You don't have to spend *beaucoup* money for an employee recognition program to succeed. Instead, simply use your creativity, thoughtfulness, and effort.

> *You don't have to spend* ***beaucoup*** *money for an employee recognition program to succeed. Instead, simply use your creativity, thoughtfulness, and effort.*

If you already have employee recognition programs in place, determine if they actually *motivate* your employees in positive ways. I mean, really; just how many paperweights and coffee mugs do you think it takes to motivate your workers?

Is your reward system based on years of service? Unfortunately, these systems have become associated with "staying power" rather than actual performance. In effect, people receive a badge of honor that says "I survived."

Do you have an Employee of the Month program and does it actually get results for you? If you have *beaucoup* employees from whom you select one a month, guess what? You leave out a majority of employees. After you take into account the fact that you don't want to select the same employee twice, you could end up scrambling to name someone who hasn't yet received the award (usually because he or she hasn't actually *earned* it).

Also, consider what happens when one program works well with one team member and fails miserably with another. For instance, my friend Julie has worked for her company for 20 years. Her employer is organizing a luncheon at which she'll be recognized for her years of service and called forward to receive a certificate of appreciation. She plans to skip the whole thing, saying this public demonstration would make her *honte* (embarrassed). She'd much prefer a quiet, private acknowledgement of her dedication. On the other hand, her co-worker, who's expected to receive a service award at the same luncheon, looks forward to it immensely. She'll probably arrange to have her whole family attend. How effective is this one-size-fits-all approach to employee recognition?

Whatever techniques you use, your goal is to develop a workplace culture of recognition for performance.

A generic employee recognition program doesn't fly. Make the effort to determine what most inspires *each* of your employees. Whatever techniques you use, your goal is to develop a workplace culture of recognition for performance.

Successful Employee Recognition

So what's the key to successful employee recognition? It's simple (and it works with your spouse, friends, and family, too). Simply get to know the individuals and find out what they like. Ironically, it's the simple forms of sincere personal thanks that still have the greatest meaning.

For most team members, the way they're treated every day matters more to them than tangible rewards. That communicates appreciation.

Top-ranked techniques that influence employees (based on their own lists) include:

- providing the information people need to do their jobs,

- getting employee input on decisions (especially those affecting them),

- asking employees for their opinions and ideas, and

- showing support when they make a mistake.

Add to that the following: a choice of work assignments, flexible work schedules, training and professional development opportunities, and accessibility to their managers.

Also consider choosing from this list of informal recognition options to reward your team members for good performance:

- extra time off from work

- preferred parking space

- public, verbal, email, or voicemail praise

- written thank you notes (test and see how effective this one can be!)

- movie, restaurant, car wash, coffee, or entertainment gift certificates

- customers' letters of appreciation posted on the bulletin board or intranet

The most effective way to recognize and reward team members is to make your acknowledgments timely and meaningful—and delivered with a personal touch. Keep *chacque á son gout* in mind. Some like it hot and others simply don't!

Find a Neutral Ground

As legend has it, in the mid-19th century in New Orleans, a schism developed between the French who lived in the French Quarter and the Americans who lived on the Uptown side of Canal Street. The median on Canal Street that separated the two became a non-conflict area between the two "armies" that was controlled by neither side. Eventually, farmers set up stands in that neutral ground, and residents from both sides could peacefully buy their fruits, vegetables, and coffee there. .

The term has stuck. Although a neutral ground is no longer needed as a safe zone for French Quarter residents, New Orleanians and others throughout South Louisiana still use the term "neutral ground" to describe the median of any two-sided street.

Neutral Ground at Work

At times, do you need to establish a neutral ground in your workplace?

"I just don't *get* him," complained James, a participant in my workshop as he described a co-worker. "Max is the most difficult person I have ever worked with!" He went on to explain how Max made it tough for him to get needed information and made no effort to cooperate.

An exercise I use in my workshop calls for talking about characteristics and interests we have in common as well as identifying unique individual qualities. When people discover shared hobbies and experiences, it gives them a neutral ground for building a stronger relationship.

Doing this exercise spurred James to redouble his efforts with Max. He later reported about going into Max's office to get data for a report and noticing a wall calendar that depicted a popular NASCAR racer. James asked Max about it and found out they share a passion for NASCAR racing. Hearing James's question, Max's face lit up and he became animated and enthusiastic discussing all things NASCAR. He even looked at James with newly found respect. What's more, Max has been completely cooperative ever since they discovered their neutral ground.

It just takes a little effort to break the ice. By showing sincere interest in getting to know your co-workers, team members, and customers, you're investing in building a relationship.

It just takes a little effort to break the ice. By showing sincere interest in getting to know your co-workers, team members, and customers, you're investing in building a relationship. In *How to Win Friends and Influence People,*[11] Dale Carnegie wrote about becoming more *interested* than *interesting.* That means focusing attention on the other person, not yourself, to express curiosity about him or her.

Remember, people do business with people they know, like, and trust. This doesn't only apply to customers; it goes for team members, too. When you take this approach, you find they naturally become more engaged in the organization and in their work.

So discover the neutral ground you share with those around you. Show interest in them. Find out what you have in common that you can build on. When you ask about hobbies, families, and experiences, you'll likely learn something you didn't know. You could be surprised to find out you have more in common than you ever imagined.

Ask. Don't Tell.

In my work as a leadership coach, the best advice I can give my clients is none at all. In fact, if I'm doing my coaching job properly, I'm *asking* more than *telling*.

A leader's job is much the same. Sure, you can take time to figure out your team member, Joe's problem and come up with a solution. That's often the quickest way to get him back on track. And if you have immediate answers to Joe's dilemma, why withhold them?

But you definitely don't want to come across as someone who's a *qui sait tout* (know-it-all), as we say here in bayou country. If you behave like the superhero who fixes every problem, what happens in the future? The next time Joe faces a dilemma, he'll expect you to fix it again. (This principle, of course, goes back to the Biblical proverb, "Give a man a fish and you feed him for a day. Teach a man to fish and you feed him for a lifetime.")

Taking on a coaching role requires asking Joe questions that help *him* identify the issues at hand. Then, once he researches and describes them, you ask more questions to draw out possible solutions—*his* solutions.

Remember, you're neither diagnosing nor prescribing here. Like a coach, you operate under the premise that your role is to draw out of people answers that are already inside. You're not the expert—or a *qui sait tout*—who puts in answers that were left out. That means making sure your questions support Joe in *drawing out* possible solutions. Base them on the assumption you believe Joe has the ability to solve his own problems.

What happens if you define Joe's problem for him and fix it? It's no longer his responsibility to resolve this issue. You've stripped him of owning the problem. And without ownership, if your proposed solution doesn't work, he sits back and waits for you to come up with an alternative.

Design Your Questions to Make Joe Think

Instead, set up a supportive relationship that allows Joe to take both responsibility and ownership. You do this by asking him what he *should* do, what he *will* do, and *when* he will do it. By asking these questions, you activate his motivations to figure out viable solutions.

Like a coach, you operate under the premise that your role is to draw out of people answers that are already inside. You're not the expert— or a qui sait tout—who puts in answers that were left out.

That means stay away from closed-ended questions or those that can be answered with a Yes, No, or super-short answer. Instead, ask open-ended questions that can be answered in a number of ways. Typically, open-ended questions begin with words like Who, What, When, Where, Why, or How. To avoid putting Joe on the defensive, emphasize that there's no right or wrong answer.

You'll see that your questions prompt Joe to dig deep and come up with ideas he hadn't considered before. You'll draw out of him what would have been left inside him had you told him what to do. And because Joe formulates his own plan of action, he has ownership in carrying it out. That leads to experiencing a sense of fulfilling his potential.

So ask, don't tell. Unless, of course, you want to play the superhero and repeatedly come to Joe's rescue!

Oyster Po-Boys, Pearls, and Leadership

One of the most delectable foods you can eat in our beloved Cajun country is an oyster po-boy. A po-boy is a kind of submarine sandwich that began as a five-cent sandwich for day laborers, or "poor boys."

They're still popular today, although they're not available for five cents! You can get your po-boy stuffed with fried

Now, the word "conflict" evokes a negative meaning, particularly conflict in the workplace. But it isn't necessarily negative.

oysters, shrimp, fish, soft-shell crab, crawfish, well you get the idea. Oh, *mae cher,* my mouth waters just thinking about it!

But watch out! Don't be surprised if your teeth crunch down on a pearl. (No need to worry about pearls if you're slurping down raw oysters on the half shell without chewing. Your teeth will be spared. And talk about good!)

Pearls form when a piece of grit, sand, or shell gets trapped inside the oyster. It protects itself from irritation by secreting a liquid around the particle. Eventually over time, the secretion builds into what becomes a pearl.

How interesting that an irritant can be the catalyst for creating something beautiful and valuable.

Managers tell me they spend a large part of their workday settling conflicts among their employees. Now, the word "conflict" evokes a negative meaning, particularly conflict in the workplace. But it isn't necessarily negative.

Like the beautiful pearl comes from an irritant in the oyster, something valuable often comes from conflict. It actually turns positive when it challenges people to explore new ideas, sparks curiosity about differences, or stretches the group's problem-solving efforts.

Certainly, conflict among co-workers is inevitable, and managing it within a work group can challenge even the best leaders. Your job? To channel the energy around a conflict for the greater good of the team. Let me explain.

Two Types of Conflict

Let's boil down workplace conflict into two types: One is a difference of opinion on directions, decisions, actions, and ideas—or "substantive" conflict. The second is known as a "personality clash" or "personalized" conflict, a fancy way of saying two people just can't—or won't—see eye to eye.

Substantive conflict usually crops up when dealing with work-related issues and *can* be a positive thing. If handled properly, co-workers can resolve a disagreement with a creative solution that improves on each party's original position. Rather than approaching the issue as "one solution wins over another," both individuals focus on solving the problem in a new way. They bring to the table their own ideas and create a solution using both points of view—what business guru Stephen Covey calls synergy, or the whole being greater than its parts.

Boy, if all workplace conflict could be that easy!

Unfortunately, as you probably know, most workplace disagreements fall into the second category: personalized conflict. While substantive conflict can be positive, personalized conflict, well, not so much, because emotions such as anger and frustration enter into the mix.

Personalized conflict proves difficult to resolve because individuals focus more on the other person than on the problem itself. In addition, they dwell on their preconceived ideas rather than on the facts and objective problem-solving tactics.

*Remember that while you may have no direct control over another person, you do have control over yourself. When you bring attention to the **issues**, not the **personalities**, you encourage the others to do so as well.*

What's the solution? When dealing with personalized conflict in the workplace, get those involved to focus on specific issues. Remember that while you may have no direct control over another person, you do have control over yourself. When you bring attention to the *issues*, not the *personalities*, you encourage the others to do so as well.

Addressing Conflict

As a leader or manager, you're probably faced with playing referee between two or more of your employees—a complaint I hear often! While I'm certainly not a relationships expert or counselor, I've had *beaucoup* experience in this department (unfortunately).

Therefore, I've put together these few *bon mots* (pearls of wisdom) to help you support your employees in resolving conflicts with as little bloodshed as possible:

- Encourage individuals to get their emotions under control and gather their thoughts before they say something they'll regret. The only decisions that can't wait are those involving the safety or health of an employee. You can put off all other decisions until facts are gathered and emotions are checked.

- Train your team members (and yourself) to use active listening skills. That is, restate what the other person says before responding. Listen to the whole message rather than only what you want or expect to hear.

- Foster an open-minded work culture so individuals realize *their* way is just *one* way of looking at things. Instead of asking, "How can I win?" encourage them to ask, "What can I learn?"

- If team members must criticize, get them to criticize *ideas,* not *people.* Focus on the issues instead of blaming or insulting others, which only results in destructive conflict.

- Urge team members to ask questions rather than assume. You know the saying, when we assume . . . . Well, you can only guess what others think or what motivates them.

Yes, it's all easier said than done. But your goal is clear: To help your team members learn to work out disagreements on their own.

Hey, if all else fails, take everybody out for oyster po-boys. Just watch out for the pearls!

Fired Up! Or Burnt Out?

Are your team members Fired Up! about their jobs? Or are they Burnt Out?

These days, employees are constantly pressured to do more with less, but some feel the effects more than others.

Friends and colleagues tell me they see more disengaged employees today than ever before. Dubbed "The Walking Dead" by many management experts, they go through the motions of work, doing the absolute minimum to get by.

Now, as you read that description, I'm willing to bet you pictured a specific co-worker or team member. Yep, at least one person around you has burnt out, checked out, and pooped out. And yet, he or she is still taking up space on the job. (Please say it's not you!)

Sadly, most disengaged workers were usually once engaged, enthusiastic, productive workers. At one time, they approached their jobs, as we say here in bayou country, *á bon couer,* or whole-heartedly. Why have they become so discouraged?

Well, disengagement typically begins with a change in the workplace—a new boss, a new assignment, a new location, extra duties, or a combination of these. More commonly, though, people get disengaged because they receive little or no support from their leaders. Those nearing the point of burnout haven't minded pulling extra weight, but they want acknowledgment and appreciation

Those nearing the point of burnout haven't minded pulling extra weight, but they want acknowledgment and appreciation from their bosses for it. Without that recognition, why bother staying engaged?

from their bosses for it. Without that recognition, why bother staying engaged?

Sadly, these less-than-stellar employees stay with your organization only as a *pis aller,* or last resort. They simply can't or won't find another job. Why do leaders need to be concerned about disengaged employees? Because their lack of effort eats into the organization's profitability and success and can also break the spirits of co-workers.

In addition, disengaged workers are more likely than satisfied employees to—

- be less productive,

- have accidents,

- cause errors big and small,

- provide poor customer service, and

- have a record of absenteeism and/or tardiness.

Tactics Leaders Can Take

Okay, before this gets *you* totally depressed, let's address what you can do as a leader to prevent disengagement—and even *re-engage* those on their way to the check-out counter.

Show your love! Let team members know how much you appreciate their efforts. A little bit of recognition goes a long way.

Treat employees as individuals. A one-size-fits-all approach to leadership just won't cut it. Honor individuality and modify your leadership approach to each person. (Remember, *chacque á son gout!*)

Create a greenhouse for your employees to grow in. Provide vital opportunities for your team members to continue learning and honing their skills.

Make employees feel like partners. Clue them in to the big picture. Let them know the rationale behind what they're doing so they can take pride and ownership in their work.

Pay attention to top performers. Your "stars" are always the first to leave if they become discouraged. Fully acknowledge and appreciate their efforts. Sometimes just having you notice they did their job with pride can reignite their spirits.

Deal with poor performers quickly. Stop the spread of the "disease" before it infects your top performers (and everyone else). When a leader ignores the poor performance of one worker, the morale of others drops. Don't let that happen.

Respect your employees. Everything you do as a leader can boomerang back to you. If you treat people with respect, you'll likely be treated with respect in return. Besides, it's the right thing to do.

As a leader, you have tremendous influence on those around you. Simply letting your team members know you're concerned about them can be enough to curtail an impending Burn Out and even get 'em Fired Up!

C'est La Vie

In case you haven't heard, here in South Louisiana, we love our crawfish!

During the spring, the height of the crawfish season, we have as many crawfish boils as we can fit in, and we cook crawfish in a million different ways. *Ooh, mae cher, ca c'est bon!*

But my favorite is to have an outdoor crawfish boil, where we cook them seasoned just so in a big pot over a burner. When they're done, everyone gathers around long tables covered with newspapers. These bright red, steaming hot mudbugs are poured out onto the center of the table and everybody digs in.

They say that before the Acadians came to live in Louisiana, they used to eat lobster in Acadie (Nova Scotia). After the people were exiled, they traveled down the eastern seaboard and eventually settled in Louisiana. The story goes that the lobsters followed the Acadians, but as they made this long journey, they became smaller and smaller. In this way, the crawfish—along with the robust, hearty Cajuns—adapted to their new home.

Cajuns Adapted and So Can You

"That's the way we've always done it!" Boy, if only I had a nickel for every time I've been told this when I asked, "Why do we do things this way?" Mama always used to say, "Nothing is constant but change! *C'est la vie*—that's life!" As Cajun history shows, she meant that adapting to change is a necessary part of life.

People, I have found, tend to be creatures of habit; they resist making changes in their routines, work, and lifestyles. Some, though, resist more than others. It seems that every work group has a team member or two whom others tiptoe around, carefully avoiding their turf and their etched-in-stone procedures. These people resist change even if it's a change for the better—one that makes their work more efficient or leads to better customer service.

Two Approaches

However, I'm not advocating change for the sake of change. Let me cite two different approaches to deal with the same situation.
A new manager has just been hired to run an already successful business. As soon as he arrives, he enforces a new dress code, new reporting procedures, and new attendance rules. He even insists his staff give him weekly activity reports—something new for them. What message is he sending? "Good thing I've come along to correct your mistakes and get this business on the right track!"

What happens? The formerly cheerful, congenial staff starts grumbling and groaning about the new regulations and procedures. Employee morale drops to an all-time low; so does overall productivity. The employees spend more time talking *about* their boss than they do talking *with* him. This manager, not understanding the problem, tightens the reins and micro-manages every business activity. Not surprising, the morale problem worsens.

Now picture a new manager who comes into a similar situation with an entirely different approach. This manager's first order of business? To meet with staff members and praise them for their previous successes. He also thanks them for their loyalty and asks for their support as he learns the ropes. He holds off making changes in procedures; he wants to first get a feel for what works and what doesn't. With any employees who resist his leadership, he asks for their help or assigns them special projects. Because of that, they feel respected and valued.

Comparing these two vastly different styles, you'd be surprised how many times new managers come in impos-

In a light-hearted, non-threatening way, we drew out their concerns and fears, and we put to rest issues that were limiting their productivity. It led to genuine acceptance of this new manager by his team members.

ing the first approach and then wonder why their staff feels resentful. (As a consultant, I've observed this many times.)

I was once hired to deal with a situation like this. I advised a new manager to take the second approach and hold off making wholesale changes. Then we gathered the team (including the new manager) and I facilitated teambuilding sessions for the group. In a light-hearted, non-threatening way, we drew out their concerns and fears, and we put to rest issues that were limiting their productivity. It led to genuine acceptance of this new manager by his team members.

Tread Lightly

Even if you're not a new manager, it's wise to tread lightly when implementing changes in your organization. Here are a few tips to help you.

- **Make sure the change is necessary.** Don't change a policy or procedure just because you think *your* way will be better.

- **Focus on a vision.** Helen Keller once said, "Nothing is more tragic than someone who has sight, but no vision." Connect with team members to develop vision and mission statements so you're all working toward a common end. Post your goals where employees will see them frequently, helping them stay focused.

- **Get input from your team members.** I can't emphasize this enough. When you're initiating changes that affect their work, ask for their opinions. Chances are they'll point out flaws in your proposal and offer better ideas. What's more, by asking for their suggestions, you'll get greater buy-in for the changes you implement.

- **Give and receive feedback.** Offer correction or praise as soon as possible so team members can make adjustments right away. Also be open to their concerns and criticisms by asking them how they think things are going and what they would do differently.

- **Lead by example.** Although this seems obvious, you'd be surprised how many managers subscribe to the "do what I say, not what I do" philosophy. Don't be one of them.

- **Acknowledge employees and reward their progress.** Recognize small achievements and frequently reward team members for their effort and commitment.

- **Expect the road to be bumpy**. Not everyone happily jumps on the bandwagon for change. Some will resist and even seek to sabotage your efforts. Use your creativity to handle or diffuse any impending conflicts.

C'est la vie! Mama was right. Nothing in life is constant but change. Yes, everyone has to deal with it.

Remember, as a leader, how you approach change influences how your team members adjust to it—and that ultimately affects customer satisfaction, productivity and profits.

Create Your Own "Bayou" GPS

Waterways play an important role in South Louisiana—from the Mississippi River to the lakes, ponds, and ever-present bayous. Settlers naturally established towns and communities along the bayous, building their homes and businesses on the *batture,* or the high ground on the banks of the bayous. In fact, Bayou Lafourche is often called "the longest street in the world" because folks used the bayou for transportation and to make their living.

The bayou has always been used as a point of reference when giving directions. Today, if you ask people how to get to a certain location, they'll likely tell you to go "up the bayou" or "down the bayou" or "across the bayou." Yes, for us in bayou country, it's our natural GPS.

But knowing this didn't bail me out one fateful day. I must've made at least 10 u-turns and I still couldn't find the location of my meeting. After a frantic call to my husband and his search on Map-Quest, I finally located the place, and then I vowed to purchase a GPS as soon as the meeting ended.

Okay, I admit that even with a bayou nearby, I'm directionally challenged. So I have my GPS now and, though I'm not a gadget person, I'm loving this tool. All I have to do is plug in the address of my destination and let it plot my route. Regardless of what wrong turns I may take, what pit stops I make, or what opportunities for retail therapy I partake in, it keeps me on the right path.

Isn't that the job of a leader, too? (Stick with me on the logic here; I know where I'm going this time!)

Leaders Keep Others on the Right Road

First of all, as a leader, you need to always have in mind the big picture—the ultimate destination and direction you're supposed to be heading. Like a GPS, you keep your team members on the right road regardless of any side trips and detours they may take.

Know what's really cool about my GPS? When I make a wrong turn or miss one, the voice doesn't yell at me in exasperation or tell me I've screwed up again. Instead, its oh-so-pleasant voice chimes in and says, "In 100 yards, make a u-turn." Really, a simple nudge is all I need.

Similarly, your team members might also need that nudge to get them headed in the right direction. Berating, shouting, and criticizing them only serves to fluster them, even demotivate them.

Remember, part of your job is to help them develop their skills. When babies learn to walk, you don't yell and criticize them for falling. No, you gently pick them up and set them moving again.

Certainly, your team members will fall from time to time, especially when trying out new skills. They'll naturally look to you to set them straight. That's when you gently and patiently guide them in the right direction.

Don't Wait; Provide Ongoing Feedback

The day I made the 10 u-turns (okay, I exaggerated *un peu*), I'd passed by the building and didn't even know it. But my GPS would have given me feedback about where I was in relation to my destination.

Your team members want—and even *crave*—feedback. They like to know where they stand. Sometimes giving them so-called bad news beats giving them no news at all. Who looks forward to their performance appraisal time anyway?

Because of my background in human resource management, I constantly coach managers and supervisors to give their employees ongoing feedback. If they're doing great, let them know. After all, what gets acknowledged, rewarded, and celebrated gets repeated. (And yes, even if they're just "doing their job," acknowledge them often!) Now, if they need a nudge to get back on track, give it to them. But for good-

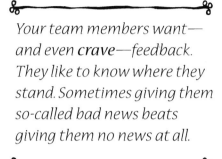

*Your team members want—and even **crave**—feedback. They like to know where they stand. Sometimes giving them so-called bad news beats giving them no news at all.*

ness sakes, don't watch an employee make the same mistake for six months and wait until the annual performance appraisal to provide feedback. (You wouldn't believe how many managers do this!)

I know the job of leader, manager, or supervisor can be frustrating. But I also know first-hand how rewarding and fulfilling it can be. So keep your eye on your ultimate destination and remember the value of having your own brand of GPS. Sometimes all that's needed is a gentle nudge and a u-turn or two.

Just a Ti Na Na . . . or Not?

In Cajun French, a *ti na na* is a fussy person - someone who complains a lot, often over trivial matters. They bring complaining to a whole new level. Know anyone who fits that description? Raise your hand if they're in the cubicle next to you! Well, *mon amie,* you have my condolences.

One day as I was getting all caught up on my Facebook Friends' lives, I noticed an all-too-common complaint in the posts. It seems everyone who commented suffers from Monday Morning Mourning. They dread going back to work after a wild weekend, or a relaxing vacation, or whatever they just experienced. One friend even posted this: "Monday morning . . . I detest you!"

Pretty strong stuff! This pattern leaves me wondering if these people are just a bunch of *ti na nas* who enjoy getting sympathetic responses (and attention). Or are they really *that* disengaged with their jobs? Surely the level of lethargy they convey isn't legit. Or is it?

Find Out Who Dreads Mondays and Why

Now, I'm not saying people should always skip off to work glad that the weekend has ended. But this business of hating Mondays seems intense—and could be problematic.

What do *your* team members say about Monday mornings? Take time to ask them. Understand what they think and feel about coming to work. Here's a *bon mot* from Mimi (my maman or grandmother): "*Mae cher*, you'd better be careful what you pray for (or ask for) because you just might get it!" That means think twice before "friending" them on Facebook to find out their true feelings. When you do, you may just get the truth, the whole truth, and nothing but the truth—and there may be nothing constructive about it!

What you want is constructive feedback, not complaints.

As a leader, you realize that simply sending your people home with a paycheck doesn't necessarily keep them coming back for more. And it certainly doesn't do much to get them fired up every Monday morning. Employees can't live on paychecks alone and, as the adage says, money can't buy happiness.

So if you suspect that your team members engage in Monday Morning Mourning, you've got your work cut out for you. Start by examining the kind of culture and work environment you've created. Are you investing in your people? What can you improve?

So if you suspect that your team members engage in Monday Morning Mourning, you've got your work cut out for you. Start by examining the kind of culture and work environment you've created. Are you investing in your people? What can you improve?

The Four "I" Factors

Practicing the following four "I" factors might encourage your team to feel eager about returning to work on Mondays.

- **Independence.** No one wants to feel like Big Brother is watching, and most people like having freedom in how they work. Giving employees latitude increases the chance that they'll perform up to snuff. To nurture their independence, make it easy for them to offer suggestions for better ways to get their jobs done.

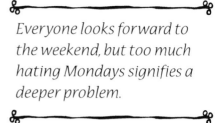

Everyone looks forward to the weekend, but too much hating Mondays signifies a deeper problem.

- **Involvement.** Involving team members in decision-making—especially when the outcome affects them directly—is both respectful and practical. Plus, those closest to the problem often have the best insight on what works well. More than that, involving others increases their buy-in, which in turn helps ease the way when implementing changes.

- **Information.** Team members want to know how they're doing in their jobs and how their contribution fits into the big picture. Tell them how the company is doing in the marketplace and share what you think the future holds, bringing them "in" to a wider conversation. It matters!

- **Interesting work.** Some jobs are just, well, flat-out boring. But to the degree you can provide opportunities for team members to vary their routines, learn new tasks, or cross-train in other jobs, do it!

I believe people come to work with the intent to contribute to the organization, not to be *ti na nas*. It's up to you as a leader to get them—and keep them—engaged in that intention. Sure, everyone looks forward to the weekend, but too much hating Mondays signifies a deeper problem.

If you see Monday Morning Mourning among your team members, what are you doing about it?

Beware the 'Gators!

It's no secret that the bayous and swamps of South Louisiana are full of alligators. Alligator hunting in the area has become well known in America thanks to TV shows like *Swamp People* (on the History Channel). Alligators can grow to anywhere from 9 to 13 feet in length and weigh up to 500 pounds. Imagine how a critter that size can do damage!

When I was a kid, our family regularly went to Lake Verret and spent the entire day water skiing. (I still love to water ski, though I don't do it much anymore.) Naturally, my parents cautioned us to look out for alligators.

I don't need to tell you that alligators are fierce predators with jaws so powerful, they can crush hard-shell turtles. What's interesting, though, is that they're sneaky and quiet—until they attack, that is. They move soundlessly through the water. Often, what you might identify as logs floating in the water turn out to be 'gators quietly watching you. They may be silent, but they sure are deadly.

As a leader, you've no doubt had the "pleasure" of dealing with an employee who is *difficile,* or difficult. (If not, count yourself lucky.) I've certainly had to deal with my fair share of "difficult" co-workers as well as subordinates, and I hear this complaint from leaders often.

You know the ones; they even have names. The Complainer (aka the *Ti Na Na*) the Gossip (aka the *Commere),* the Bully (aka the *Brute)*, the Green-eyed Monster (aka the *Jalousie*), the Sneak (aka the *Canaille*)—and the list goes on. You can probably add a few of your own.

Like the alligators in South Louisiana, these "difficult" people have the ability to attack and ravage your workplace without you even seeing them coming.

What Motivates "Difficult" People?

Unfortunately, I don't have a one-size-fits-all solution for this problem. I will say this, though. To deal with "difficult" people effectively, understand what motivates them to act the way they do. More often than not, "difficult" people act as they do because they can—and because their unwelcome behavior has worked for them in the past. That's how they gain control over situations and other people.

As their leader, you always have the choice of ignoring their unwanted behavior. I must warn you, though; you could wind up losing your top performers and customers as well as your credibility and the morale and respect of other employees. Like the alligators, ignore them at your own peril!

Another choice is to hold firm, no matter how tough it might be, until their behavior gets corrected. You simply don't have to play on their terms! Consider your measured reaction and attitude toward these "difficult" employees to be your best defenses. Do your best to keep them under your control.

When I conduct workshops for leaders, I remind them to address the negative behavior itself, *not* the person doing the bad behaving. By maintaining this focus, you avoid getting personal and exacerbating the problem (as well as falling into a possible trap).

Ways to Address Unwelcome Behavior

Don't let bad behavior drag on unaddressed for very long or the damage done to the morale of the rest of the team could be irreversible. Start with these tactics:

Expect a positive outcome, no matter what the history has been. Your expectations will shape your nonverbal communications, which in turn can affect the outcome. I know, it's easier said than done. But generally, what you expect in other people is what you get. So expect a positive outcome.

Be direct, descriptive, and non-judgmental. Remember; go after the *deed*, not the *doer*. Be careful not to judge; you don't know everything going on in the employee's life that contributes to the behavior.

Address the facts, not gossip or rumors. Confirm any secondhand information. You have to seek out the source of the gossip before you can deal with it.

Be aware of your body language. Maintain steady eye contact when communicating with a "difficult" person. Watch your tone of voice and timing. Avoid being accusatory or argumentative.

Mentally plan your approach in advance. Allow enough time to make sure you don't blurt out something you'll regret.

Ask questions instead of using explanations. In your conversations, ask the "difficult" employee what he or she can do to solve the problem at hand.

Be clear in your communications. Don't expect people to read your mind. Instead, tell them what you expect from them.

Keep trying fresh tactics. If one idea didn't work in the past, it makes no sense to keep doing it expecting different results (the definition of insanity).

If none of these tactics works, you might have to conclude this "difficult" person simply won't change.

Ultimately, though, you can only be responsible for your own actions and how you allow the behaviors of others to affect you. As the one charged with putting an end to behavior that disrupts and undermines the team, simply do the best you can.

Well, I told you I had no magical, one-size-fits-all solution to the problem of the *difficile* employee. But I do have this word of caution: Always look out for these silent but deadly predators. Like the alligator, they'll strike when you least expect it.

Leadership Lagniappe

Different people have different tastes, so to explore other ways of *Modifying Your Approach to Season the Conversation,* go to

http://www.ledetmanagement.com/freeresources

Bring Out the Best in Others with Respect ("The Stock")

Bring Out the Best in Others with Respect

The Stock

By now, our gumbo is stewing with the Cajun Four Seasons doing their flavoring magic. It's time to add good rich stock to our creation.

Because we're making seafood gumbo, we use a heavy stock-pot and throw into it our crab shells and shrimp peelings as well as onions, garlic, bell pepper, celery, and maybe even some carrots. Basically, we use whatever we have on hand minus the kitchen sink. Then we cover these ingredients with water. (I add liquid crab boil to give it a little more spice—but that's a personal preference.)

Next, we'll let this stock come to a boil and simmer for a while. Once we've extracted all of that good flavor, we strain it and add it—ladle by steaming hot ladle—to our gumbo pot.

This rich stock helps all ingredients come together—to "marry" as they say—without competing with or overpowering each other. We don't want our seasonings to *blend* together per se; rather, we want each ingredient to retain its unique flavor while contributing to the rich flavor of the completed dish.

Team Members Retain Unique Flavors, Too

When you have a diverse team, you experience conflicts, frustrations, and misunderstandings due to differences in style and approach. Yet having mutual respect and appreciation for each other's differences, talents, and strengths enables each member

Having mutual respect and appreciation for each other's differences, talents, and strengths enables each member to retain a unique flavor while contributing to the strength of the team—like the seasonings in the stock.

to retain a unique flavor while contributing to the strength of the team—like the seasonings in the stock.

Interestingly, the very person who drives you nuts is probably the one you need to have right beside you. For example, if you're an outgoing, engaging person who's disinterested in details, you'd do well to have an analytical, detailed person at your elbow. These strengths complement each other! Of course, your differences can create friction, too—that is, *if* you don't recognize, value, and respect the strengths the other person brings to your whole team.

In the Cajun culture, extended families get together often. Someone who's a distant cousin in other cultures is considered a close relation in South Louisiana. Our predominantly Catholic population leads to large extended families. With gumbo on hand, if unexpected guests drop in to eat, we simply add more stock to make the gumbo stretch!

In the same way, you can bring together a rich, diverse team with different styles, personalities, strengths, and values. They'll work well together, providing you have *beaucoup* respect for one another.

The people in South Louisiana have descended from French, Spanish, African, and German and other traditions. A mix of ethnic backgrounds flavors our gumbos and other wonderful dishes we enjoy today. Ingredients and spices from different nationalities have been folded into our recipes to enhance the flavors of our already delicious dishes. Like a good gumbo, we come together to create a rich, spicy, flavorful culture like no other in the world.

Why not do something similar in your organization? Don't think in terms of *tolerating* the differences of team members but rather of respecting, valuing, and celebrating the spicy flavors each individual brings to your team.

What Leadership is All About

As a leader, your role isn't necessarily to "put in" what was "left out" of your team members but to draw out what was "left in." When you focus on their strengths rather than their limitations—when you value each individual's input—you help bring out the best he or she has to give.

> *Don't think in terms of tolerating the differences of team members but rather of respecting, valuing, and celebrating the spicy flavors each individual brings to your team.*

What's more, when people are allowed to work in their area of strengths, they add value to the organization. Consequently, they feel happier and more fulfilled.

Your customers will benefit from this strong stock—respect— and so will your entire organization.

Ya Gotta Be Nice to People!

In the Cajun culture, children are raised to respect their elders, and as an adult, regardless of age, you continue to exhibit that respect. In fact, you might call any number of people "Aunt" or "Uncle" (or *Tànte* or *Nonc)*, even if the person is your older cousin, a close family friend, or not related at all. You would use "Mr." or "Miz" before the first name of any friend of your parents or anyone older in the community even if *you* are 70 years old! (My daddy had a friend nicknamed Knucklehead. To this day, we call him *Mr. Knucklehead!*)

After my Cajun father-in-law loudly pounded the table to get our attention, he used to say, "You gotta be nice to people! Nobody likes a *chu* (an ass)!" Okay, so he was no Plato. But his little *bon mot* holds true, not only in personal relationships but also as a vital part of leading effectively.

Vicious Cycle of Incivility

When was the last time you read a credible study that said rudeness, incivility, and sarcasm are the best ways to treat employees to get maximum productivity from them? *You know that ole dog won't hunt!* When employees are forced to deal with bullying from their boss and co-workers, you can bet their work suffers. And no doubt their productivity and efficiency suffer, too.

I can't tell you how many people I've heard complain about

their rude, insensitive, demanding bosses and co-workers! Or how many times I've heard, "He just doesn't know how to talk to people!" But what happens? Rudeness and incivility breed more rudeness and incivility. It's contagious like a wildfire. When people are on the receiving end of this type of treatment, they tend to dish it back—and the vicious cycle continues.

In the workplace, incivility can turn into downright harassment. Now, I'm not talking about sexual harassment, racial discrimination, or workplace violence. I'm addressing downright lousy behavior that can include yelling, bullying, using sarcasm, barking out orders, sabotaging the work of another, and just not using the manners our mamas taught us (or should have taught us!).

Never ignore rude behavior just because it's not legally labeled "harassment." General rudeness can, in fact, support a claim of hostile work environment or sexual harassment, especially if the plaintiff can prove the behavior was gender-based.

Besides the potential legal problems, rudeness and poor manners can affect your team's productivity. A survey of 775 employees who were the victims of workplace rudeness showed that 53 percent lost work time worrying about the rudeness, 46 percent thought about changing jobs to get away from the instigator, 37 percent felt less committed to their employer, and 28 percent lost work time trying to avoid the instigator. (Participants were allowed to check off more than one response.)[12] Research has also shown that more than one-third of employees surveyed had quit their previous employers because of their supervisors' undesirable behavior.

Most companies fall down when it comes to selecting and training their managers. Often an employee is promoted to a managerial position without proper preparation for the job. And many leadership development programs focus only on the technical aspects of management, neglecting to provide training in the area of people skills. Indeed, I've come across managers who relish the opportunity to tell workers, "You'll do it because I said so, that's why!" Yes, some leaders are tyrants, plain and simple. They rely on people to put up with their rude treatment because the employees need their jobs.

Yes, some leaders are tyrants, plain and simple. They rely on people to put up with their rude treatment because the employees need their jobs.

Create a Kindler, Gentler Workplace

So what can you do to avoid being known as Atilla the Hun, the Wicked Witch of the West, or a *vilain* of your workplace? The following is a list of do's and don'ts to help you create a kinder, gentler workplace.

Do—

- always tell the truth.

- think before you speak.

- practice the Golden Rule.

- say "please" and "thank you."

- listen carefully to what people say.

- be conscious of your tone of voice.

- deliver on the promises you make.

- feel free to admit your own mistakes.

- treat all people with dignity and respect.

- be diplomatic and delegate with dignity.

- include others in decision-making processes.

- spread credit and compliments to all who helped.

Don't—

- be a perfectionist.

- interrupt other people.

- avoid taking responsibility.

- get personal or belittle anyone.

- bark orders like a drill sergeant.

- be antagonistic or negative.

- point the finger or play the blame game.

- use sarcasm, yell, stomp your feet, throw things.

- jump to conclusions before you have the facts.

- make excuses when something doesn't work the way you wanted.

Every day, practice the adage "You'll catch more flies with honey than you do with vinegar" and the Golden Rule: "Do unto others as you would have them do unto you."

Add to these the simple *bon mots* of my father-in-law: "Ya gotta be nice to people!"

A Shot of Tabasco Goes a Long Way

Our very red Golden Retriever named Tabasco has been a part of our family for 11 years and counting. If you've ever known the joy of owning a Golden Retriever, then you know how eager to please this breed is.

When we first got Tabasco as a puppy, my husband and boys wanted to train him for hunting. I had no objection because I knew from experience with our first Golden that training him would make for a very obedient pet.

By the time Tabasco was a year old, he'd been officially trained for duck hunting and, as expected, he was obedient. I realized early on that once he'd been trained to obey, he could be taught anything. So my big contribution was teaching him to fetch my morning newspaper. Okay, I don't have a great future as the next famous Dog Whisperer, but I felt proud for teaching him this task.

However, I quickly learned that the retrieving part wasn't the hard part; it was bringing it back to *me*. So every time he returned the paper to me and let me take it (after I said thank you, of course), I'd rub his ears. (Goldens love to have their ears rubbed.) I also rewarded him with a piece of cheese.

Now, Tabasco's Mama didn't raise a *Cooyon* (fool). He figured that if he got praise, an ear rub, and a piece of cheese for one newspaper, he'd be completely pampered if he brought back two or three newspapers!

You guessed it. Each time I praised him, he looked for something else to bring to me. To this day, if I don't watch him carefully, he'll retrieve my newspaper, my neighbor's newspaper, and any other newspapers he finds on the block. (My dear neighbors know to ignore the dog slobber and teeth marks by now!)

Yep, a little praise goes a long way with Tabasco. Have you ever noticed how far a little praise goes with people too? The more I acknowledge my family members for desirable behaviors, the more eagerly they repeat those behaviors. Don't be surprised if employees respond to your positive reinforcements in the same way.

> *The more I acknowledge my family members for desirable behaviors, the more eagerly they repeat those behaviors. Don't be surprised if employees respond to your positive reinforcements in the same way.*

People, Like Dogs, Love Praise

Now I'm not saying you should use dog training techniques to enhance your people skills, but this praise thing does work with almost anybody—subordinates, team members, family members, and yes, of course, dogs. Most people are like Tabasco in that they are—deep down—eager to please. The more they're praised for a certain behavior, the more likely they'll repeat it.

The experts call it positive reinforcement. It means when you see a behavior you want repeated, you praise and even reward the individual who did it. (Cheese or a dog bone works well for Tabasco; I suggest you find out what your teammates like and offer that instead!)

Here are a few powerful steps you can take to develop the habit of congratulating instead of criticizing.

Catch people doing something right and/or doing the right thing. Yes, you can train yourself to be more tuned in to the positive. When you spot something praiseworthy, let 'er rip!

Be sincere and specific. People see right through false praise and ooey-gooey mush. Be real and genuine with your praise. Explicitly tell people what they did that you appreciate.

Don't take others' efforts for granted. Even when they're just doing what's expected of them, acknowledge their dependability and dedication. Sometimes you may have to reach deep to find something good to recognize. Even if you can simply commend them for showing up for work on time, do it.

Give a handwritten note or card. This goes a long way and costs very little. How many times have you seen a personal card or note pinned to a team member's bulletin board or standing up on the desk? Because everyone gets so many emails, your handwritten card stands out in the crowd.

Set a goal to recognize a specific number of people each day. This alone will push you to constantly look for the positive.

Give *yourself* kudos. Celebrate your own wins and accomplishments. Reward yourself once in a while.

These techniques not only work to acknowledge team members. Use them with your managers, co-workers, friends, family members, and even your dog. A shot of praise—like a shot of Tabasco in your gumbo—goes a long way.

A Little Lagniappe

In South Louisiana, we often use the term *lagniappe*, which has both Spanish and French roots. (Remember, Louisiana has been under both Spanish and French rule, so many of our terms derive from those languages.) *Lagniappe* historically referred to a little something extra a friendly shopkeeper might add to a customer's purchase. Literally translated, it means "to give more."

Cajuns use *lagniappe* today to mean an extra gift or benefit—a bonus—while folks in other parts of the country might use the term "baker's dozen" to mean the same thing.

I like the idea of giving more. If only we could each adopt this as our personal philosophy and practice! In customer service and sales, the application of this term is clear: to give more than is expected. In my business, I have made it a practice to under-promise and over-deliver, with the emphasis on over-delivery.

> *In customer service and sales, the application of this term is clear: to give more than is expected.*

Here's an example. For my family's California vacation, we enlisted the help of a travel agent who booked hotels, advised us about driving distances, and recommended sights to see. Yes, he was compensated for his efforts, but as a little *lagniappe*, I put together a Cajun gift basket and sent it to him. He never expected it and was totally floored by this thoughtful gesture.

As a leader, can you give more? Can you provide a little *lagniappe*?

Giving More...

Yes, you can always give more, including more of these possibilities:

- **Respect** for others. Acknowledge that differences in behavior, style, and approach are, as Martha Stewart would say, "A Good Thing." Appreciate that we each have strengths that add value to the team.

- **Time** to mentor and teach. Share your wisdom, knowledge, and experience to help someone grow and learn.

- **Trust** in your team members. This is perhaps one of the toughest things to give as a leader, but probably the most empowering for your team members. Mentor, teach, guide, give feedback, and then trust them to get the job done their way.

- **Attention** to what people are saying. That means listen more and talk less. Hear what's being said as well as what's not being said. (Yeah, so you might have to peel your eyes away from your smartphone for a few minutes.)

- **Empathy** for another's circumstances and struggles. Take your focus off yourself and tune in to the other person. Empathy is the ultimate virtual reality. Put yourself in another person's shoes.

- **Feedback** to team members. They would rather receive negative feedback than no feedback at all. Please tell them how they're doing!

- **Consistency** in your actions and behavior. Your team members need to know what to expect from you day in and day out.

Lagniappe is a way of life in South Louisiana, a part of this glorious culture. As a leader, you can make it part of *your* organization's culture.

I believe that the more you model the practice of giving a little *lagniappe*, the more positive results you will see from your team— and the more positive experiences your customers will have. Ultimately, it adds a wealth of value to your organization's success.

Reap a Sweet Harvest

Where I come from, sugarcane is king! In fact, sugarcane—the highest-valued row crop in the state of Louisiana—has been an important agricultural product for more than 200 years. Sugarcane first came to Louisiana in 1751 with the Jesuit priests, who planted it near their church in what's now downtown New Orleans. The sugarcane industry has continued to grow and flourish in our area through the centuries.

We recently spent the weekend with friends at historic St. John Plantation in St. Martinville, Louisiana—a working plantation with a sugar mill right next to the centuries-old home. Picturesque moss-draped oaks line a circular drive, the big white house features verandas front and back, and the sweet smell of raw sugar hangs in the air. We visited in October—the thick of grinding season— when the cane is brought to the mill for processing. I love watching the cane trucks and wagons deliver the harvest to the mill. (Of course, I'm watching from the comfort of the veranda with an adult beverage at my side, so I find the scene both entertaining and fascinating.)

Imagine for a moment you're a sugarcane farmer with the opportunity to farm acres and acres of land. Your equipment can harvest all of your acreage and you have the potential to make a huge profit.

Would you farm and harvest only two of your fields and let

the other two fields go to waste? *Alors Pas!* (Of course not!) Would you harvest all four fields but only send the cane from two fields to the sugar mill for processing? Not likely. You would farm, harvest, and fully process all four fields, getting the maximum benefit/profit from these resources.

Are You Drawing Out the Max?

In business, why would you deal with your people any differently? Leaders often fail to draw out the maximum possible benefit from their greatest resources, their people. To reap your best possible harvest, just as with sugarcane or any other kind of crop, you've got to willingly put in the work up front before you realize a harvest.

I'm not a farmer (although I did own Farmer John overalls at one time). But I've put together a few tips based on farming terms to help you cultivate a banner crop among your team members.

Soil. To grow anything successfully, farmers know to start with nutrient-rich soil. As a farmer, you till and prepare your land long before you begin planting. You want to provide the proper foundation for your crop. In business, you also need to provide a proper foundation and plan for success. Identifying and establishing your area's mission, vision, and values is like preparing the soil for your team members. Telling them the intended growth plan makes it richer.

Seed. Farming requires you to select a crop suited for your climate and environmental conditions. Sugarcane grows best in a tropical or semi-tropical climate, making it well suited for the warm, sultry, often steamy climate of South Louisiana. Similarly, as a leader, you make wise "seed" choices in selecting your team members. Even those who seem qualified might not be a good fit, so choose your seeds well. You want to pay just as much attention to *attitude* as *aptitude* when selecting your team members. While some people may be a good fit for your organization, make sure to put them in the right roles or they won't "grow."

Fertilize. Not all of the nutrients necessary for a bountiful harvest are available from the soil, so naturally you need some fertilization. Using the right kind of fertilizer and in the proper amounts is key to nourishing a healthy crop. Similarly, as a leader, it's up to you to both nourish and nurture your team members by offering learning opportunities. Sit down and devise a development plan for all of them, allowing them to develop their strengths, explore their interests, and hone their skills.

Irrigate. If you've ever spent five minutes (yes, *minutes*) in South Louisiana, you know it tends to *mouiller* – or rain a lot here. Sugarcane, like many crops, needs proper, consistent irrigation. Although it seems counterintuitive, many cane farmers irrigate their fields due to inconsistent weather patterns and periodic droughts.

> To reap your best possible harvest, just as with sugarcane or any other kind of crop, you've got to willingly put in the work up front before you realize a harvest.

As a leader, once you've prepared the proper foundation and put together a winning team, you've got to "irrigate" your work environment to allow team members to thrive. Setting up an environment of respect and dignity is essential. So is viewing each team member as a valued individual who has much to contribute to the organization.

Harvest. Typically starting in October, harvesters cut off the cane tops and cane loaders place these tops in large wagons for transport to the sugar mills. At the raw sugar mill, the sugarcane is washed and crushed, its juice boiled down to a thick syrup. The cane by-product is bagasse, used as a fuel to power factories. This thick syrup is separated into sugar crystals (called "raw sugar") and molasses (used in livestock feed). Farmers make sure every bit of the sugarcane gets processed for a specific purpose.

As a leader, if you nurture and nourish your greatest resource, your people, you can cultivate their untapped strengths, draw out their hidden talents, and reap a strong harvest for everyone. Sweet.

Making Wise Investments

Let's play a bit. Just for fun, respond to this quiz.

- Name the 10 wealthiest people in the world.

- List six people who have won the Nobel Peace Prize.

- Name the last 10 World Series winners in Major League Baseball.

- Name those who won the Grammy for Album of the Year in any of the last three years.

Well, how'd you do? Not so hot, huh? Well, I have another quiz for you, and I think you'll have an easier time with this one.

- Name one person who encouraged you.

- Think of someone who took interest in helping you develop your skills.

- List those people who taught you something worthwhile over the years.

- Name one person who took time to answer your questions and inspired you.

I'll bet the second quiz was a lot easier, right?

My point is, the greatest leaders—those who really make a difference—aren't necessarily the most famous or notorious people around. Rather, they're the ones who make investments in their people.

Speaking of Investments . . .

When my husband and I meet with our financial advisor twice a year, he updates us on how our investments are paying us back. Before working with this advisor, we were just spending our money without any conscious thought about the long-term implications of our actions. That meant we weren't giving much thought to our future or to what we would eventually leave behind.

As a leader, when you take time to invest in people, you receive paybacks of a different kind. Your actions today create a legacy that lives well beyond your lifespan. In effect, you're making a mark that can't be erased.

> *As a leader, when you take time to invest in people, you receive paybacks of a different kind. Your actions today create a legacy that lives well beyond your lifespan. In effect, you're making a mark that can't be erased.*

The Camp

Hunting season is a big deal for many men in South Louisiana. It's almost a male rite of passage, and in our household the same is true. When our two sons got old enough, my husband began taking them to "the camp" (typically a hunting or fishing shack away from home). Now what goes on at the camp, I can't rightly say because long before Las Vegas adapted the slogan "What happens in Vegas stays in Vegas," we had been saying "What goes on at the Camp stays at the Camp." (It's okay, because I don't really *want* to know!)

What I do know is that a whole lot of male bonding goes on. *On dit* (they say) that the men hunt, tell stories, play cards (Pedro or Bourre—Cajun card games), and cook up the spoils of the hunt. Uncles, *parrains* (godfathers), papas (grandfathers), cousins, and male friends come together in this relaxed environment. The older generations "school" the younger generations in these male rituals. A common adage you'll hear in South Louisiana is this: "If you take your boys hunting, you won't have to hunt your boys." What a unique opportunity for dads to teach their boys our culture and pass down their legacies.

A Positive Legacy

What kind of lasting legacy will you leave? I suggest setting a goal to consciously leave a positive legacy by investing in others. "Investing in others" means you mentor them, take time with them, and give them your attention. No doubt, you have lots of experience and expertise. How are you transferring your knowledge, wisdom, skills, and even shortcuts to others?

When you share your experience and expertise with people, you not only help those individuals but you benefit your organization as well. When you sow seeds of encouragement, you inspire self-confidence and determination, which ultimately affects bottom-line profits.

Can you remember a coach or mentor who complimented or encouraged you? All of a sudden, your posture got straighter and you *wanted* to live up to his or her positive words. The same happens with your team members.

When you explain not only what you'd like others to do but *why* you'd like them to do it, you instill in them a sense of ownership. By seeing the bigger picture and the reasoning behind their tasks, they develop a stronger commitment to doing the job well.

Do You Model the Way for Others?

As a leader, you're always being watched! Others decide whether to follow your example or not. Mentoring can be as simple as taking time to answer their questions, enhance their skills, and patiently correct their mistakes.

Early in my career, I worked with a guy named Phil whom I've come to regard as a great mentor and coach. When I went to him with a dilemma, he rarely told me what to do. No, he'd listen and ask questions that would spark my own problem-solving skills. His questions challenged me to think with originality and doubt my assumptions. I learned a lot from him and yet he never preached, directed, or demanded a thing of me. He simply drew solutions out of me, subtly sharing his wisdom and knowledge that way.

> *I'm willing to bet that someone took an interest in you and gave you a hand or modeled the way for you. Will you pay it forward?*

As a result of Phil's investment in me, I became a highly valued team member and I know the organization reaped the benefits of my learning. Years later, I'm using Phil's techniques with people I coach. I sincerely hope I'm making the same positive difference for them that Phil made for me. I'm willing to bet that someone took an interest in you and gave you a hand or modeled the way for you. Will you pay it forward?

I challenge you to review how and where you're investing your most valuable resource—your time. Investing that time in people will bring you the most rewarding paybacks of all. Look around you. Who could best benefit from *your* time?

The Pierre Principle

ack in the late 1960s, Dr. Laurence J. Peter, a psychologist and professor of education, put forth the concept that became known as the Peter or *Pierre* Principle. (I just *had* to give it a Cajun twist.)

The Peter Principle basically states that an employee who excels at his/her position is often promoted to higher and higher positions, and eventually to one that exceeds that employee's scope of expertise. "In a hierarchically structured administration, people tend to be promoted up to their level of incompetence," Dr. Peter wrote. He even explained it in this simple way: "The cream rises until it sours."[13]

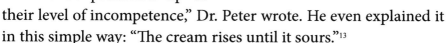

You've likely seen it happen time and again. Decisions are made to promote a high-achieving employee without considering if that person has the necessary skills to be successful in a new position.

You've likely seen it happen time and again. Decisions are made to promote a high-achieving employee without considering if that person has the necessary skills to be successful in a new position.

For example, let's say Boudreaux owns a pirogue-building company. (A *pirogue* is a small, flat-bottomed boat commonly used by Cajuns in the Louisiana marsh.) One of his employees,

Pierre (Thibodaux), is a pirogue builder—a good one. In fact, he's the BEST pirogue builder that Boudreaux has. So what does Boudreaux do? He promotes Pierre to supervisor of pirogue builders. Not necessarily a good move on Boudreaux's part. Why? Because while Pierre is quite capable of building pirogues, he doesn't necessarily have the skills to effectively lead a team. Pierre gets thrown into a position of supervising his former peers without the benefit of training, preparation, guidance, or support.

I've seen this scenario played out more times than I can count, and I'll bet you have too.

FEMA and the Peter/*Pierre* Principle

A close-to-home example of the Peter Principle became apparent in the days, weeks, and months after Hurricane Katrina struck New Orleans. With food and water in short supply and millions displaced from their homes, residents looked to FEMA (Federal Emergency Management Agency) for help. (Although I'm a big believer in personal responsibility rather than depending on government, I'm not debating that issue here.)

Now, the bumbling and bungling actions (and inactions) of FEMA provide a good learning example. Director Michael Brown, before being appointed head of FEMA, served as the commissioner of judges for the International Arabian Horse Association. (Seriously.) Because he excelled in that role, Brown was promoted to the more demanding job of FEMA director—a giant leap of faith by anyone's standards.

You know the rest of the story. FEMA was slow in providing the relief needed and did a questionable job of coordinating the efforts of different assistance agencies involved. By most accounts, Mr. Brown failed in his new role and ultimately stepped down. Now, I'm sure Mr. Brown was perfectly capable as the commissioner of Arabian horse judges, really. But how could that role have possibly prepared him to serve as FEMA's director during a crisis?

Yet I believe Michael Brown (or any high-achieving team member) could make a great leader—if given proper preparation, development, and mentoring. As a leader, it's your responsibility to make sure your managers and supervisors get the tools and ongoing support they need to succeed.

> *Supervisors need someone with whom they can confidentially discuss delicate personnel issues and air their concerns. That's support.*

Importance of Ongoing Support

Why is ongoing support in leadership development important? Because anybody who's been there can affirm that it's lonely at the top. Supervisors need someone with whom they can confidentially discuss delicate personnel issues and air their concerns. That's support.

So maintain an open door for your managerial staff to do just that. Otherwise, your supervisors might feel like you've thrown them into alligator waters to sink or swim. Give them a lifeboat (a *pirogue* will do) and be there for them. Don't forget to take advantage of teaching/coaching opportunities. And of course set the right example by being a good leader and mentor for them.

Will Rogers once said, "Everybody is ignorant. Only on different subjects." Like Pierre, supervisors don't automatically know how to supervise, but they *can* learn. And in a competitive business environment, good bosses are key to employee productivity and retention.

Therefore, doesn't it make sense to invest time and money to train your leaders well—so they don't fall victim to the Peter/*Pierre* Principle?

Zen-Like Leadership

In a recent conversation, my friend Heather described her daughter's horse training experience—something new for me. (My kids participated in anything that involved a ball so we didn't have the time or energy to add horseback riding to the mix.)

> One trainer described the process as "harmony without coercion." That's why it's important to establish a bond of respect early on.

What she shared with me was very interesting, and I was struck by the fact that many of the principles of horse training correlate to leadership. She described it as a very Zen-like activity.

CC, Heather's daughter, spent much of her early training doing the groundwork necessary to establish a relationship with the horse before ever attempting to ride it. She said the most difficult task to teach a horse is forward motion. Of course, if you can't get the horse to move forward on command, you also can't get him to trot, run, or jump, so it's *trés* important.

Moving Forward

If you were the trainer or the leader, you'd teach the horse to move forward using gentle signals with a rod. First, you'd *ask* the horse to move forward by showing the rod. Then you'd *encourage* the horse to move forward by gesturing with the rod. And finally, you'd *tell* the horse to move forward by *touching* him with the rod. (Notice I didn't say by *hitting* the horse over the head with the rod.)

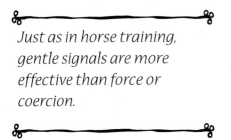

Just as in horse training, gentle signals are more effective than force or coercion.

In horse training, the trainer/leader keeps in mind that strength isn't determined by force but rather by technique, confidence, and another critical factor—creating a bond of respect. (Sounding familiar?)

One trainer described the process as "harmony without coercion." That's why it's important to establish a bond of respect early on. A horse who respects you feels at ease while being attentive to your commands. He understands that if you discipline him, it's for good reason. Gradually, he learns to trust you in the event of perceived threats in the environment.

Any time the horse is intimidated by you rather than respects you, he will act *de peur* (in fear) that you might act out against him. Of course, if the horse fears you, he won't trust you when there's a threat in the environment. Indeed, he can become confused when you discipline him, especially if it's done inconsistently or frequently. He could get spooked or even flee and leave you stranded.

How true this can be, both in horse training *and* in leadership!

Environment of Respect, Not Fear

Yes, the old "command-and-control" style of leadership *il a mouri* (has died)—for good reason. To get others to follow your lead in a Zen-like way, you have to first invest time to build relationships with them. If you want to entice someone to take action and move forward, using force won't get you very far for very long.

Working in an environment of fear and intimidation causes people, as it does horses, to *tracasser*—that is, get worried and be distracted. When they're afraid, you can forget that they'll be creative in any way.

In the same way, anxious, stressed-out employees are prone to having accidents, making mistakes, providing poor customer service, and ultimately checking out and becoming disengaged.

After establishing a foundation of respect and trust, a Zen-like approach means treating your employees with dignity and honoring their efforts. You earn their respect every day through your consistently respect-full actions.

Just as in horse training, gentle signals are more effective than force or coercion. Naturally, at times, you need to be direct—like yelling "Stop, Drop, and Roll!" if an employee's clothes catch fire. But other than true emergencies involving potential loss of life and limb, pledge to approach employees in a Zen-like way—with respect and a gentle signal.

Leaders who practice this know they can count on team members to be there when the chips are down. And employees who feel valued and respected won't spook their leaders and leave them stranded.

As the Team Turns . . .

ike sands through the hourglass, so are the days of our lives . . . .
Is your workplace culture like that of a daytime soap opera? Do new workplace *zoombarah* (dramas) unfold every Monday morning? Are spats between co-workers the norm?

Do you often hear a musical crescendo in the background?

If so, then your workplace culture has got the *maladie,* or is as sick as the plots on *General Hospital.* I'm afraid it's not a make-believe disease, nor can it be cured in a 30-minute episode. You just may be suffering from Toxic Team Syndrome!

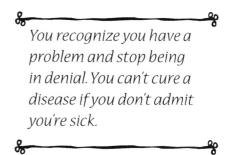

You recognize you have a problem and stop being in denial. You can't cure a disease if you don't admit you're sick.

Toxic Teams and Leaders

I often come across toxic work environments that have the *maladie.* Although it's tough to diagnose your particular problem—I'm no doctor and don't even play one on TV—but I'm willing to bet these problems are merely symptoms of leadership failings and missteps like these:

- Lack of vision from leaders,

- Poor communication between leaders and team members,

- Failure of leaders to develop their staff, letting boredom take over,

- Use of a one-size-fits-all approach to recognition and rewards,

- No emphasis/effort on creating a positive work culture,

- Forced competition among team members (an oxymoron),

- Lack of awareness of how leaders affect their team members, and

- Focus on managing processes, tasks, and systems, not mentoring, engaging, or inspiring team members.

Want the good news? It's not fatal if you catch the symptoms early. First, you recognize you have a problem and stop being in denial. You can't cure a disease if you don't admit you're sick.

12 Steps to a Cure

Yes, I believe that *you* create a healthy work environment. If yours resembles a dramatic soap opera, you can correct it by following my 12-step program for detoxifying your workplace.

Step #1. Leadership is an inside job. Identify your own strengths, limitations, blind spots, etc. Lead from a place of self-assurance and confidence.

Step #2. Treat each person as an individual but don't play favorites.

Step #3. Don't participate in or tolerate malicious workplace gossip. Establish a professional atmosphere in which all team members are treated with respect.

Step #4. Reward, recognize, and encourage teamwork and avoid setting up situations that require team members to compete against one another.

Step #5. Ask for and listen to feedback from team members, customers, and superiors. Then make changes where needed.

Step #6. Provide team members with relevant development opportunities and cross-train them when it's appropriate.

Step #7. Clue people in to the organization's big-picture dreams; share your own vision for its future.

Step #8. Explain to each team member how his/her work contributes to the vision.

Step #9. Err on the side of over-communication. Great leaders know they can't overdo communication with their team members.

Step #10. Get to know team members and focus on drawing out the best they have to give. Serve as a mentor, guide, and inspiration to them.

Step #11. Strike a balance between setting yourself above (and superior to) your team and being one of the gang. Somewhere in the middle is best.

Step #12. Work hard to build and maintain both trust and loyalty. And *never* discuss one team member's issues, problems, or situation with another.

Remember, you only have One Life to Live! So do your best to detoxify your own work environment for the benefit of All My Children.

To Get Good People to Stay, Just Ask!

So what if your employees quit? Can't you just replace them? Sure you can!

But don't be such in a hurry. Studies show the cost of replacing key employees runs between 70 and 200 percent of the worker's annual salary.

Consider these reasons why you should care about employee retention:

- Losing an employee costs between 6 and 18 months of that position's pay. You'll probably have to advertise and recruit, then spend time interviewing. If you're lucky enough to find a qualified replacement, you then have to find time to train the new employee.

- Managers, professionals, and hi-tech workers can cost twice as much as other employees to replace. Plus, it takes considerably more time to recruit, hire, and train a replacement for those positions.

- You have to take into account hidden costs such as losses in productivity, customers, and sales.

Given this, why aren't more leaders applying employee retention strategies? Because of time. Many leaders/business owners find their businesses run *them* rather than the other way around. They don't have time to find out what their exiting employees wanted that might have enticed them to stay. Unfortunately, they're asking the burning questions during the exit interview instead of when they could still make a difference.

Ask These Two Burning Questions

You don't have to devise a complicated strategy for finding out what your employees want. All you have to do is *poser deux questions—* that is, start with these two simple questions:

- What makes you want to stay here?

- What might lure you away?

Dit mon la verite! (Tell me the truth!) Be prepared, of course, to carefully take in their answers. Keep an open mind and be careful not to poo-poo their ideas. As you listen, don't make promises and also don't say how unrealistic their suggestions might be.

In fact, you might be delightfully surprised at the range of answers you'll get when you ask. Most managers believe that money is the one and only motivator keeping their employees with the company. Do you fall into this category? If so, you're putting the burden of keeping employees on your pay scales. But in reality, *you* have more power than anyone else to keep your team members from leaving. Research bears out this truth.

Top Reasons Employees Stay

Depending on which study is referenced, the following items usually appear (in varying priority) among the top reasons employees stay with a company. They are:

- Positive relationship with boss/supervisor,

- Recognition for work well done,

- Opportunities for learning, training, and career advancement,

- Exciting and/or challenging work,

- Decision-making authority and control over their work,

- Feelings of being "in" on events within the organization,

- Meaningful work that makes a difference and a contribution,

- Fair pay and benefits,

- Leaders who inspire them, and

- Positive work environment/culture.

When you ask each employee "what makes you stay and what might lure you away?" note their answers and decide if you can influence that person. Review your notes monthly and assess what you've done for him or her. If you want to ask more questions in the form of a satisfaction survey or a focus group, let your employees submit their responses anonymously. You might hire a professional to collect and analyze the responses for you.

> *Start with these two simple questions:*
> - *What makes you want to stay here?*
> - *What might lure you away?*

But really, it doesn't matter how you do it. The most important thing is to *poser des questions!*

If you believe you don't have this time to invest in your team members, think of it this way: If you ignore these important assets—your people—then don't expect to keep them on board.

Crabs in a Champagne

One of my favorite summer pastimes is crabbing off Grand Isle, Louisiana's only sandy beach. Louisiana boasts some of the most delicious blue crabs ever, and I enjoy catching them almost as much as I enjoy eating them.

When we go crabbing, my husband and I pack an ice chest with refreshments, bait our nets, and set out in our little *Jeaux Boat*. As we catch the crabs, we put them in what we call a *champagne*, which is a plastic basket with no cover that allows water to drain.

If you've ever observed crabs in a champagne (or a bucket or barrel), you know that if there's only one crab in it, that crab will have no difficulty getting out. But when there are multiple crabs in the champagne and one tries to get out, the others pull it back down.

This same principle holds true with people. Ever feel like you work with a bunch of crabs in a champagne? When adversity strikes, you may try to maintain a positive outlook, but there will always be someone who dwells on the negative and tries to pull you back down. It's like the sign at our camp that reads, "Life's a beach. Watch out for the crabs!"

Staying Positive

Picture this. Seven-day cruise, Caribbean Sea, middle of November, getaway for a group of friends. Sounds delightful, I know.

Before we left, my friends and cruising mates expressed concern about a hurricane supposedly heading in the same direction as our cruise ship. I'd been looking ahead to this much-anticipated vacation and simply didn't want to hear about a possible hurricane disaster. In total denial, I refused to watch the weather forecasts and continued packing my bathing suits and sunscreen.

When I'd gone on a cruise several years ago, I'd worried about getting seasick. At the first little ripple in the water, I took seasickness medicine. (I know now that seasickness is about the power of suggestion.) Determined not to get sick on this cruise, I'd convinced myself I'd be fine. Hurricane or not, I would *not* get seasick! Instead, my goal was to drink lots of water, exercise (fairly) regularly on-board, get fresh air—and look at the horizon any time I felt the least bit queasy. Mind over matter.

In the rough seas of today's economy, people are tempted to wring their hands and moan about how bad things are. Now, I'm not naive enough to believe you can ignore the "weather" reports and wish bad news away. Instead, I suggest you focus on what you *can* do for your organization rather than what you *can't* do. Take a mind-over-matter approach.

As a leader, you have a responsibility to guide your ship through the stormy seas. That means encouraging your people to stay positive and focus on the possibilities. If you mope around spouting gloom and doom, exactly who are you helping?

How to Draw Out Their Best

Even if today's business challenges become increasingly difficult to manage, realize that your job calls for innovative solutions to stay competitive. Your main role? Draw out the best that each employee has to give.

Start by following these tips to guide your people through today's turbulent waters:

- Clearly communicate the current situation to your employees,

- Share the forecast/outlook for your organization with your people,

- Frequently ask for their input to implement programs for solving problems,

- Challenge all employees and staff members to be proactive, not reactive,

- Confirm your commitment to them and to the organization while requesting their commitments, and

- Be resourceful and creative!

Encourage your team members to give all they've got to your organization and make their efforts known. To get that result, they can:

- demonstrate their value to the organization by becoming a problem solver,

- show their dedication and loyalty by going the extra mile,

- stop pointing out the obvious challenges and come up with solutions (by not being crabby!),

- strive to work well with others as a team player, and

- consistently and genuinely approach work with a "can-do" attitude.

Henry Ford once said, "Whether you think you can, or you think you can't, you're probably right." I strongly believe in this principle because it reflects the power of a positive outlook.

By the way, I did *not* get seasick on that cruise and we did *not* encounter the forecasted hurricane. In fact, I have no idea where it went. I never watched the weather reports.

Remember our sign's message. "Life's a beach. Watch out for the crabs!"

Patron Saint: A Game Plan for Leadership

No guarantees. In fact, nothing was certain about Drew Brees' move to New Orleans as the new quarterback for the Saints (our beloved National Football League team). Hurricane Katrina and her aftermath had devastated the city of New Orleans and the Gulf Coast. They both looked like a war zone. City leaders considered tearing down the Superdome and even moving the team to San Antonio, Texas.

But Drew Brees was up for the challenge—and he proved to be an integral part of rebuilding not only a team and a sports organization but an entire city.

Drew performs countless hour of service to the community, whether wielding a hammer to help build houses with Habitat for Humanity or visiting children in the hospital.

I remember the first home game the Saints played in the Superdome after Katrina, September 25, 2006. It was against the Atlanta Falcons. My husband and I attended this historic game that still gives me *frissons* (goose bumps) when l when I think about it. I'd never witnessed so many people crying and laughing and celebrating at the same time. Even Atlanta fans hugged us!

This symbolic game showed the world the city of New Orleans and its people would recover. And recover they did. In the years that have followed, Drew Brees and his wife, Brittany, continue to

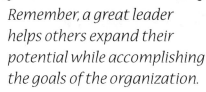

Remember, a great leader helps others expand their potential while accomplishing the goals of the organization.

help their adopted hometown get back on its feet.

Brees has certainly awed fans with his on-field leadership and ability, but his leadership abilities extend well beyond the playing field. Drew performs countless hour of service to the community, whether wielding a hammer to help build houses with Habitat for Humanity or visiting children in the hospital. With humility and respect, Drew gives back.

When it comes to his teammates, Drew has a reputation of being selfless. He sees his role as an encourager, someone who makes it possible for others to succeed. "What makes a man is the ability to sacrificially *give* while expecting nothing in return. What makes a leader is someone who's willing to die to self every day for the benefit of the team. Drew has that down pat," said Heath Evans, a Saints fullback who, with his wife, hosts weekly Bible studies for the team at their home. "He's always team-focused instead of Drew-focused. That is the make-up of a true leader."

Servant Leadership

That's also the heart of servant leadership. Now that's not a new concept. In the sixth century B.C., the ancient Chinese sage Lao Tzu talked about selflessness and service. In Christian Bible stories about Christ's life, Jesus urged his followers to become servants first. Most world religions—even agnostics and atheists with strong morals and high ethics—support the concept of servant leadership.

But isn't that idea a tad too soft and fuzzy in tough, demanding business environments? In a competitive, results-oriented marketplace, is there value in putting other people first? Doesn't a servant leadership approach suggest weakness?

In actuality, some of the toughest, most successful leaders have practiced servant leadership, and that includes Herb Kelleher, former CEO of Southwest Airlines. Why not give it a chance to thrive in *your* work environment?

Servant leadership means serving your team members first—developing, empowering, and supporting them. Remember, a great leader helps others expand their potential while accomplishing the goals of the organization.

Of course, to be a servant first, you have to be humble yourself. No leaders who regard themselves as superior to others can be servants. As an aspiring servant leader, you must be able to put yourself, your needs, and your demanding ego aside. Truly being effective means placing your focus on service instead of control and self-interest.

In multiple ways, Drew Brees serves his team, his organization, and his city. He helped rebuild an organization; plus he taught a team what it means to win and a city what it means to hope.

You might not be called on to do all that, but you *are* called on to serve—your team, your organization, and your community—ahead of yourself.

Leadership Lagniappe

Some like hot, others like mild, so to
discover more ideas for *Bringing Out the
Best in Others With Respect,* go to

http://www.ledetmanagement.com/freeresources

Optimize Influence

("The Meaty Part")

Optimize Influence

The Meaty Part

Cajuns possess a certain *joie de vivre* (love of life) that's engaging and energizing. They're well known for their rich culture, their strong sense of community and family, and their lively spirit. Add to that their fierce determination and ability to rise up and thrive amid myriad challenges, and you have a model for effective leadership.

> *Like a Cajun host, it's up to you to fill your workplace culture with respect, cooperation, and collaboration. Indeed, it influences the success of your team.*

Go into any Cajun home and you'll find the door always open. Unexpected company is, indeed, expected. You'd be welcomed in a warm, friendly way because Cajuns love people and they also love to *veiller* (pronounced *vay yay*)—visit. You're encouraged to pull up a chair and listen to their lively tales, some taller than others.

Bienvenu á notre maison, my friend.
We lift our glasses high.
Come taste the gumbo in the pot,
And the crawfish in the pie.[14]

Cajuns create a warm, welcome environment. As a leader, you also create a culture and work environment through your influence. You set the tone and determine what is and is not accepted, recognized, and rewarded. Like a Cajun host, it's up to you to fill your workplace culture with respect, cooperation, and collaboration. Indeed, it influences the success of your team.

Core Substance: Your Positive Influence

As you know, your ability to influence the actions and performance of people—to get the work done through others—is key to being an effective leader. In making gumbo, this core substance is represented by the seafood or the meat. In effect, it's the protein source of your gumbo.

Protein gives your body strength. Similarly, your ability to positively influence your team members provides the strength needed to not only withstand challenges but to flourish through them.

Here in South Louisiana, we understand that challenges are inevitable. After all, we've faced devastating hurricanes, damaging oil spills, and disastrous downturns in the economy. And we've proven our resiliency and strength each time.

Positive influence requires understanding the basics of motivation. Consider these points:

You *can't* motivate other people. This may seem counterintuitive, but it's true. It's not about "putting something in" that was left out. And that's because . . .

All people are already motivated. Each person gets motivated by his or her own needs, goals, and fears. These internal motivations drive action from within.

People do things for their own reasons. Which, by the way, may not be the same as *your* reasons. So what does a leader actually have the power to do?

You *can* create an environment in which people feel self-motivated to achieve their goals. Through the culture you create, you tap into their internal motivations and influence their behavior.

In a nutshell, everyone gets motivated by something—and that something lies inside them. Good leaders find out what motivates their team members and make environmental changes that feed

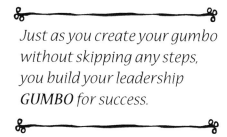

Just as you create your gumbo without skipping any steps, you build your leadership GUMBO for success.

those motivations. Ideally, the resulting cultural environment gives them permission and support to leverage their strengths, maximize their assets, and give the best they've got to the organization.

In today's business climate, team members—

- expect respect,

- crave contribution, and

- appreciate leaders who inspire and engage them.

This is the "meaty" part in your leadership recipe; it's where the gumbo comes together. Just as you create your gumbo without skipping any steps, you build your leadership GUMBO for success.

And remember to add your unique flavors and spices. Talk about good, *cher!*

Influence and Savoir Faire

If I had to define leadership today in only one word, it would be "influence."

Notice I said "leadership today." The principles of leadership in the 21st century differ greatly from those in decades gone by. What might have worked 25 years ago would never fly today. The old "command and control" leadership style implied, "You'll do it because I'm the boss."

In contrast, leadership today requires *influencing* employees to perform and produce at their highest capabilities for the greater good of the

> That means when you lead through influence, people follow you. They perform and produce because they **want** to, are compelled to, and are inspired to do so.

organization *and* for their own fulfillment. No sign of manipulation; even the word "persuasion" is too strong to describe the kind of influence I'm talking about.

Defining Influence

Influence is defined by *Encarta* this way: "The power that somebody has to affect other people's thinking or actions by means of argument, example, or strength of personality." *Merriam-Webster* defines it this way: "The act or power of producing an effect without apparent exertion of force or direct exercise of command."

That means when you lead through influence, people follow you. They perform and produce because they *want* to, are compelled to, and are inspired to do so. They don't respond to you solely because of your title or position. Lots of influential people have no title at all, while some in high positions are powerless to get results through others because they can't influence them. (You know who they are.)

> Perhaps it takes experience, a few missteps, and even a bit of maturity, but a highly influential leader can learn to master the art of *savoir faire*.

Your influence, of course, must be both positive and constructive. I'm sure an argument could be made that Hitler was an *influential* leader. But he used his well-honed influential power to do evil by turning to manipulation, coercion, and control. It's the leaders who positively focus on *others* (not themselves) who wield tremendous influence.

The Power of *Savoir Faire*

The French (both Cajun and Parisian) expression *savoir faire* means having the ability to say or do the right thing gracefully—an integral part of being influential. And influential people who help, serve, and inspire others *attract* people who want to be part of their team.

Those with *savoir faire* can quickly survey a situation and the people involved, then respond graciously and orchestrate the desired results. Some call this an instinctive ability with which only certain people are blessed, but I believe it can be learned. Perhaps it takes experience, a few missteps, and even a bit of maturity, but a highly influential leader can learn to master the art of *savoir faire*.

I hate to sound like an old *maman,* but I believe that maturity and a few trips around the block have a lot to do with *savoir faire.* I've seen young inexperienced leaders rely on their titles too much to influence others. Their intent? They want to maintain control over situations and people. But remember, you can't control others, and in fact, the more you try, the less influence you actually have.

While you can't *control* anyone except yourself, you can *influence* people through your ability to say and do just the right thing at just the right time. By modeling *savoir faire* well, you influence others with class!

Coach to Win in Business, Too

Did you play sports back in the day? I didn't (shocking to learn, I know!). But since my three kids have played practically anything that involves a ball, I've spent my fair share of time in the bleachers as a spectator. And I didn't know that my TV actually catches programs other than Sports Center!

While watching my kids play sports, I especially enjoy observing their coaches. They fascinate me because the really good ones can get players to perform in ways that even the players themselves didn't know they could do.

Great leaders do that, too. If you think about bosses or leaders who influenced you tremendously, I'll bet they, too, served as coaches eager to win.

Why should you, as a leader, strive to be a great coach? Because business, like sports, is a team effort. To succeed, each player/team member has to give his or her best. Good coaches/leaders draw that out of them.

Why should you, as a leader, strive to be a great coach? Because business, like sports, is a team effort. To succeed, each player/team member has to give his or her best. Good coaches/leaders draw that out of them.

Take Cues from Successful Coaches

Outstanding coaches/leaders not only have technical knowledge of the game/business, they practice the proven principles that follow.

- Each "player" has unique talents that need encouraging. What a waste not to capitalize on each person's natural abilities and assets.

- A word of praise goes much further than criticism or negativity. Sometimes you have to look hard to find something to praise, but it will be well worth your effort. At least acknowledge their hustle or their perseverance. (Can you remember a coach or mentor speaking words of encouragement to you? All of a sudden, your posture got straighter and you *wanted* to live up to the positive comments. The same happens with your team members.)

- You can't motivate someone else, but you can inspire them to want to contribute to the team. People get motivated for their own reasons

- Losing one game or making one mistake doesn't make the player a loser. Strong coaches use temporary setbacks as teaching moments.

- Getting to know each player's life off the playing field helps you not only build a relationship but improves how you communicate. A little empathy can go a long way!

- Sharing the credit for team success builds everyone's self-confidence, pride, and trust. In fact, nothing destroys a team member's trust faster than seeing the leader take credit for the team's ideas and accomplishments.

- Successful coaches/leaders know they must first "show the way" for their team members. They are being watched!

Are you an outstanding coach for your team? Can you use practice in this area? Be prepared, though. Serving as a great coach gives you as much (or more) in return as you give to your team. You all play to win!

Super Bowl-Style Leadership

New Orleans. January, 2006. Blue tarps on almost every roof. Cars washed up onto demolished houses and apartment buildings. Only a smattering of restaurants and stores open for business.

When Sean Payton made his first trip to New Orleans to interview for the head coach position with the New Orleans Saints football team, the city hadn't yet caught its breath after Hurricane Katrina had blown through. Needless to say, this once-thriving, vibrant city-turned-ghost-town and disaster zone didn't look like it was "ready for some football."

But Payton was up for the challenge with all it entailed. In fact, he and his wife, Beth, looked at this opportunity as a calling to serve.

Are you familiar with how the Saints rose out of the devastation of Hurricane Katrina to the top of the football world in 2009-2010? Except for the team's eternally loyal fans in Louisiana and the Gulf Coast, how it unfolded might seem surreal to outsiders.

I still get the *frissons* (goose bumps) when I think about the Saints' Super Bowl miracle win – and still get choked up talking about it today. You see, my daddy had season tickets since the very first Saints season in 1967. My father-in-law was a die-hard Saints fan even when people were putting bags over their heads and calling them the "Ain'ts". But most people in Cajun Country have rooted for the Saints ever since that first season.

What Exemplifies a Great Leader?

Now, as you may know, I am no sports aficionado. However, I know a strong leader when I see one, and Coach Sean Payton of the New Orleans Saints exemplifies a great one. Whether you're a Saints fan or not, you'd learn a lot by taking a page out of Sean Payton's leadership playbook.

See where you'd rank yourself on this list of qualities modeled by Payton.

Inspire a vision. Coach Payton arrived at the Saints organization in 2006, less than a year after Katrina, when this city in shambles desperately needed something to be happy about. He used his influence to bring in quarterback Drew Brees and instilled in the team a vision to play in the Super Bowl. He held that vision for both the players and the fans. In the Super Bowl XLIV game, he made thousands of people happy by achieving that goal.

Get out of the way. You've heard the expression "Lead, Follow, or Get Out of the Way." One of the most important things coaches can do is to let their players do what they do best. Nothing kills motivation and initiative faster than micromanaging team members. Sean Payton knows when to get out of his players' way.

Create a winning environment in which others feel a personal responsibility to give their best *and* know that their contribution matters. Coach Payton tells every player the importance of the role they play to the success of the team.

Breed other leaders. Great leaders inspire confidence and bring out the best in others. I firmly believe that a leader's purpose is not to create more followers, but to create more leaders.

Show humility. Coach Payton was quick to give credit where credit was due, mostly to his players. Then he showed great humility and graciousness in dedicating the famous Super Bowl win to the Saints fans and to the city of New Orleans.

Trust your team members and inspire their trust in return. Great leaders have one thing in common: They trust and inspire trust. Indeed, leaders who don't trust their team members operate from the old "command and control" management philosophy. That usually results in players performing properly as long *as the leader is present to enforce it* but slacking off the minute the leader's back is turned. As I've heard it said, "If you trust in others, you will be trusted in return." Sean Payton places a great deal of trust in his players and coaching staff. That's why they have a personal desire to perform their best.

Give gentle nudges when needed. In the 2009 NFL playoff game against the Minnesota Vikings, young kicker Garrett Hartley (only 23 years old) was about to kick the final field goal for the Saints. Making that field goal meant winning the game. Coach Payton calmly told Garrett to focus on hitting a small fleur-de-lis on the façade of the second deck that was dead center between the uprights. He also expressed confidence in the kicker's ability. He didn't yell about the importance of that field goal; he didn't tell Garrett he *had* to make the field goal; he didn't remind him of his missed 37-yarder in a crucial game against Tampa Bay. Rather, he calmly gave his place kicker a gentle nudge. What happened? Hartley made the field goal and the Saints won the game in overtime, paving the way for their subsequent Super Bowl victory.

Under the leadership of Sean Payton, the Saints won the Super Bowl for the first time in franchise history. Whether or not you're a Saints fan (and why wouldn't you be?), you can learn valuable leadership lessons from this Super Coach.

Ah, Duct Tape!

I can't remember ever having a repairman come to our house in all of my years growing up. My daddy could fix anything!

Once in a while, though, when Daddy came across a thorny problem (like reattaching the head of my favorite doll after my brother decapitated her!), he reached for the ever-handy duct tape. Yes, my favorite doll had a "choker" made of duct tape for the rest of her life!

Daddy just used some good old Cajun ingenuity. The Acadians, aka Cajuns, had plenty to adapt to when they first came to this strange land of Louisiana. They learned to be make-do cooks and make a living by whatever means they could (although I don't think they had duct tape way back then!). Generation after generation has lived this legacy. I believe we can learn important lessons from them today.

Don't you wish you could just reach for the duct tape when your work team is coming apart at the seams? In one teambuilding activity I use in my programs, I lay out two long strips of duct tape side by side on the floor, sticky side up. Then we form two teams of about six people. Team members stand on the strips of duct tape, one behind the other, and, moving as a team, they "walk" across the room as if they're cross-country skiing. The team that travels farthest within the time limit wins.

Sounds simple, but it can be challenging—and a lot of fun!

What's Needed to Succeed?

The requirements for success in this activity mirror these requirements for a group of individuals to function well as a work team:

- **A common goal.** If each individual tried to go his or her own way, people would be pulling in opposite directions and there'd be a lot of falling down on the job. Does your work team have a clear, common goal, or does each individual take off in his or her own direction?

- **A leader.** Whether by official designation or by unofficially stepping forward, one person takes charge at the head of the line. Do you have a team leader, or is it every man (or woman) for him/herself?

- **A plan.** If one person starts off on his right foot and the next person starts off on her left foot, nobody goes anywhere except maybe down. Similarly, does your team plan its work in advance, or do you just get moving and then react? Do the team members understand how the steps taken today will bring them closer to the team's goal tomorrow?

- **Clear communication.** Each team member must communicate what he or she needs to meet the goals. Are you clearly communicating your needs and actively listening to what your teammates say?

- **Engaged team members.** If everyone else takes the step but one person doesn't budge, an instant pile up results. But you'll still stay connected, whether you're all moving forward or all falling down. Have each member ask, "Am I pulling my weight? Or do my teammates have to push, pull, and drag me along?"

Yes, life would be easier if duct tape could put everything back together. Next time your team is falling apart, remember these principles, my daddy, and good ole Cajun ingenuity, then reach for your handy roll of duct tape (metaphorically speaking, of course)!

Highlighting a Tale of Two Leaders

I read *Highlights Magazine* as a kid and especially enjoyed "Goofus and Gallant," a feature that focused on twin boys. Goofus was the bad boy who never shared his toys, didn't use good manners, ran around with scissors, and basically did everything wrong. Gallant was his angelic twin who behaved completely the opposite. Some might call this feature corny, but I liked it.

Adapting feedback I've received from readers of my ezine and journal articles, I decided to create my own Goofus and Gallant characters,

Doofus never asks for input nor responds to his subordinates' questions or requests for guidance. Rarely does he share information about what's going on with the company.

putting Doofus and Dashing in the starring roles. From the following story, see if these guys sound like anyone you know in your workplace.

Doofus and Dashing at Work

"I just don't know if I can take it anymore!" Tim exploded in an email to me.

Once he calmed down, I got to the bottom of his frustration. Doofus (on the executive leadership team) was driving Tim crazy.

(Tim holds a high position within his organization and reports to Doofus.)

Doofus has a lofty title and excellent technical skills, but as for his people skills . . . well, not so great. He uses the Management by Spreadsheet method, focusing on tasks to the detriment of the people doing them. He closets himself in his office and issues directives via email. Doofus never asks for input nor responds to his subordinates' questions or requests for guidance. Rarely does he share information about what's going on with the company. In fact, communication with his direct reports is practically nonexistent.

> *Dashing treats team members with dignity and respect. He doesn't assume he knows it all, but rather asks team members for their ideas and suggestions. What's more, he actually **listens** to their ideas.*

Quick to point the finger when things don't go well, Doofus also swiftly takes credit for the good ideas and accomplishments of his direct reports. What's worse, he rarely engages in small talk and no one can predict his mood—fair or foul—from one day to the next. As a result, Tim and others feel disengaged and unmotivated. The last I heard, Doofus was seen running around the office with scissors and actually went swimming only 30 minutes after eating lunch!

Dashing, on the other hand, is the quintessential leader. With excellent people skills and sharp technical know-how, Dashing commands the respect of those around him. Although he may not hold a lofty position like Doofus does, he carries a great deal of influence within the company.

Dashing treats team members with dignity and respect. He doesn't assume he knows it all, but rather asks team members for their ideas and suggestions. What's more, he actually *listens* to their ideas.

Dashing is willing to roll up his sleeves to get the job done or simply get out of the way and let his team members handle projects when appropriate. He happily gives credit where credit is due. In fact, he looks for opportunities to praise his team members.

An excellent communicator, Dashing typically errs on the side of over-communicating with team members. He lets them in on the big-picture view of the organization and clues them in to changes along the way. He encourages them by tapping into their strengths and motivations.

Dashing has earned respect both within his organization and throughout his industry. In his spare time, he assists little old ladies across the street and helps his niece sell Girl Scout cookies.

Nobody can be as bad a leader as Doofus nor as perfectly angelic as Dashing, but on the spectrum of leadership with Doofus and Dashing at either end, where do you see yourself?

Come on, be honest. How would you rate your leadership influence? And what areas could you improve to become more like Dashing and less like Doofus?

The Big-Picture Aerial View

As legend has it, the Christmas Eve bonfires along the Mississippi River levee in the parishes of St. James and St. John the Baptist began in the 1800s as a way to light the way for *Papa Noel*, the Cajun Santa Claus. (Papa Noel is often depicted in his pirogue drawn by alligators named Gaston, Ninette, Te-Boy, Celeste, Suzette, and more.)

It's also said the bonfires were lit on Christmas Eve to serve as a beacon for river travelers on their way to midnight mass.

Whichever version you believe, this South Louisiana tradition of building bonfires has grown stronger over the years. It has developed into the Festival of the Bonfires with (of course) lots of food, music, and festivities. In the weeks following Thanksgiving, the levee buzzes with activity as people work together to build these elaborate bonfires designed to light the way for . . . well, you decide.

Flying in the Sky

As a kid, I believed that Papa Noel, flying high in the skies, needed those bonfires to find his way to Cajun country. Thinking about it reminds me of my recent flight in a helicopter. I loved it! I was able to see my neighborhood and familiar sites from a completely different perspective. In fact, things looked so different from overhead, I had trouble figuring out where we were. (Never mind

When you share with employees the big-picture vision, you can ignite the passion and enthusiasm they feel for their work.

that I am directionally challenged anyway!) Thankfully, the pilot pointed out known landmarks to help me out.

Most startling, though, was being able to see how erosion has affected my beloved state's coastlines. From this aerial view, it became obvious why efforts to preserve our coast are crucial to the big-picture health of our earth.

Being clued in to "the big picture" is crucial in business, too. Can you describe the overarching goals for your team and your organization? If you can't, then find out more about them and share what you learn with your team. It's important.

Are You Building Cathedrals?

Let me ask you, as a leader, do you give your team members any idea what the team and the organization itself ultimately wants to achieve? Or are your employees simply putting widgets on pieces of machinery with no idea of what they're building?

This brings to mind a popular story about three workers, recounted here because it makes this point beautifully.

"What are you doing?" a passerby asked of three workers standing beside a building under construction.

The first worker, looking tired and drained, replied, "I'm just cutting stone." (If you don't clue your team members in to the big picture, they will always be "just cutting stone.")

The second one answered the same question without enthusiasm. "Working to make a living," he grunted. (If you don't tell your team members the purpose of their work and where their contributions fit in, they'll always be "working for a living.")

The third worker, who was singing, answered, "I'm building a cathedral!" (You see, the third worker had the big picture in mind. He wasn't just cutting stone or working to make a living. Unlike his co-workers, he envisioned a beautiful cathedral where people would come to worship.)

What are you and your team members building?

Never underestimate the value of stepping back to look at the big picture. And don't forget to let your people in on the overall scheme. Even when the outlook may not be great, people prefer to know the reality of the situation than be left up in the air.

Wanting to Make a Difference Counts

Numerous surveys and studies reveal that one of the biggest sources of employee satisfaction is knowing where their contributions fit into the big-picture aerial view—the overall goals of the organization. People simply like to know they're making a difference! And if they don't feel they're contributing, then they're more likely to become disengaged from the work they do.

When you share with employees the big-picture vision, you can ignite the passion and enthusiasm they feel for their work.

My client, Stan, provides a good role model for leaders. He accepted a promotion to oversee a new division of his company. Within two weeks of taking over, he brought into his office everyone who reported to him. He told them the status of the company, where it was headed, and, most important, what his expectations for them were. Within the context of this aerial view, he explained how each person could best contribute to achieving the company's goals.

Then Stan advised his team that he'd hold these meetings twice monthly and each person would be expected to provide status reports, updating the others on their areas of responsibility. At the same time, he encouraged information-sharing among team members so they could help out each other.

Stan reported that his team members were floored by this first meeting. He also received numerous emails from them saying how much they appreciated this ongoing practice. He thought nothing of it, but apparently these team members had never felt "in" on things before. They'd never been "in a helicopter" looking at the aerial view. Most important, they felt valued by their new boss.

Never underestimate the value of stepping back to look at the big picture. And don't forget to let your people in on the overall scheme. Even when the outlook may not be great, people prefer to know the reality of the situation than be left up in the air.

You don't have to build a bonfire to light the way, but make a point of sharing *your* aerial view so your team members can feel like they're building cathedrals.

Feedback for Smooth Flying

From May 1st through November 30th each year, folks in South Louisiana and along the Atlantic and Gulf coasts stay on alert for the next dreaded hurricane that might be headed our way. South Louisiana has certainly felt the wrath of many hurricanes, so it's something we constantly pay attention to.

Meteorologists do their best to predict the path of the storm using data collected from specialized planes, satellite imagery, computer models, and radar data. They measure such things as atmospheric conditions around the storms—even those thousands of miles away—as well as employ sophisticated computer models to make their predictions. Using feedback from these tools allows them to tell the public whether to evacuate or not. This feedback is crucial to all the folks living in the possible path of the storm.

When I flew to New York, as I boarded the plane and glimpsed into the cockpit of this large commercial airplane, I was amazed by the huge instrument panel. The pilot relies constantly on this instrument panel to ensure the aircraft flies on the correct path. Of course, the pilot had already filed a flight plan with the control tower so the plane's route was clearly mapped out.

Failing to discuss performance expectations with employees in advance is like asking them to travel from New Orleans to New York without similar kinds of maps. Leaders essentially serve as navigators to the employees in their charge.

Here's what good pilots do and how you can apply these actions to performance expectations.

Map out the flight plan. Setting performance expectations is like mapping out the employee's route to success at work. This requires establishing your expectations to ensure you and the employee are tracking with the same plan. It may require you to demonstrate how the job is done, offer examples of quality work, and provide written guidelines and benchmarks for a good job. And never assume your employee knows your definition of a "good job."

Refer to the instrument panel. Throughout the flight, the pilot refers to the instrument panel to determine if the plane is on course. He'll adjust his altitude or attitude (I like that one the best!), his speed, and other measures based on this feedback. Without it and the pilot's constant course correction, the plane might easily wind up in Peoria rather than New York—or worse!

Like the instrument panel, your role is to give employees feedback on their performances—to keep them on course and give them a nudge if they veer off the route or wander off into unacceptable performance territory. Your real-time feedback charts their performance in relation to the flight plan (work performance expectations) you've already established.

Remember, most team members prefer negative feedback over no feedback at all. Wouldn't you want to have your manager tell you you're doing a job incorrectly and show you the correct way *before* you crash and burn? (Or at least before handing you a negative performance appraisal?)

Make the feedback *specific*. What good is accomplished by telling employees the 300-page document they just compiled has "lots of errors" but never spelling them out? Or that the 200-step process they just completed was done wrong? Imagine if the National Weather Service said a hurricane will hit somewhere in the continental U.S. but gave no specific locations. Frankly, it's less time consuming—and less frustrating—to give specific examples of the mistakes so people know where to correct their own course.

When some supervisors see an employee making mistakes or falling short of a goal, they don't say a word. What are they thinking—or hoping? Unfortunately, some leaders don't know *how* to give constructive feedback. Think of constructive feedback like a pilot's instrument panel. It's an opportunity to relay back to the pilot any veering off-course and suggest ways to correct it.

Most people don't get out of bed eager to do a poor job and upset their bosses. Yet without specific, constructive feedback, employees can get disillusioned, feel frustrated, and let their performance suffer. They're trying to fly without a flight plan or an instrument panel.

Remember, the feedback you give doesn't have to be confrontational. It does, however, need to be—

- timely (before the employee crashes),

- specific ("adjust this, tweak that"), and

- constructive ("you're doing a great job and simply need to course-correct").

Follow these procedures to avoid any "hurricanes" so both you and your employees can enjoy smooth flying to the *right* destination!

Anchors and Bright Shiny Objects

I admit, I'm not a serious fisherman. I like going out in the fishing *bateau* (boat) and wetting a line, but I also enjoy hanging around the boat, reading my book, working my crossword puzzle, even taking a nap. Sure, I'll cast my line once in a while *if* the fish are biting. But what's my main objective? Total relaxation!

My husband and I recently went fishing at our secret spot in the beautiful waters off the Louisiana coast. At one point, we went into shallow water where we could touch the bottom, close to the island, then threw down the anchor, jumped in, and fished around in the surf. To do this, we had to rely on this anchor or we'd lose our boat.

This led me to think about the importance of anchors when it comes to being an effective leader. "Huh? How's a leader like an anchor?" you ask. No, the sun didn't addle my brain. (It might seem like I'm jumping around but stick with my argument here.)

BSO Syndrome in Today's Workplace

There's evidence that, throughout our society, ADD (Attention Deficit Disorder) sufferers are multiplying. Not a surprise. We live in an era of information overload, 24/7 connectivity, and multiple inputs vying for our attention—so many that it's hard to absorb or retain most of what we're exposed to in any given day. Because

> *Because leaders are charged with maintaining the vision and ensuring their teams are moored to that vision, **they** become the anchors of their organizations.*

of this, employees can easily lose sight of your organization's goals and vision.

I liken this to another affliction, BSO Syndrome (Bright Shiny Object Syndrome)—a tendency to be easily diverted by new, attractive, "shiny" activities. These diversions can get people chasing interesting but unproductive endeavors. Without proper guidance, they'll continue pursuing a new venture until the next bright shiny object comes along.

Do you ever witness this or feel it yourself?

Contrast that with the need for teams to put down anchors against the storm in today's turbulent business environment. Anchors represent stabilizing factors for staying on course. Because leaders are charged with maintaining the vision and ensuring their teams are moored to that vision, *they* become the anchors of their organizations. It's their job to minimize irrelevant BSO activities that team members might chase.

Do Anchors Stabilize You or Weigh You Down?

Anchors can stabilize, but they can also weigh leaders down. Too much of a good thing is, well, too much.

Perhaps you've gone overboard (I couldn't help myself!) when these things happen:

- You get so attached to a policy or procedure that team members feel stifled and unable to try out innovative approaches.

- You run such a tight ship that employees hesitate to have

those offline conversations crucial to building strong team relationships.

- You neglect to ask team members for input on key decisions, fail to get them involved in new initiatives, and smother their development.

As a leader navigating the stormy seas ahead, strive to maintain a balance between being the kind of anchor that provides stability and the kind that drags you and your team down. Keep those BSOs at bay.

Oh, and by the way, our secret fishing spot will remain just that—a secret!

Unplug to Recharge

*S**ous l'impulsion du moment.* A spur-of-the-moment decision.

We didn't plan for it; we certainly didn't budget for it. My family's decision to take off for a 10-day California vacation became a classic *sous l'impulsion du moment.* But it's one of the best decisions we've ever made.

My mom had passed away a few days shy of her 90th birthday. I say this not to elicit sympathy but to give context to our instant vacation decision. Mama had lived a long, full life, though her quality of life at the end was nil. Her passing caused me to reflect on the good memories and think about my own family. My parents took us on awesome vacations, which were certainly part of my cherished memories. One of those vacations included an extensive trip through the state of California.

Oh, we've taken our kids on great vacations, but California never seemed to happen, despite the fact that I wanted them to experience the beauty and wonder of Yosemite and the giant Sequoia trees. With California being such a big state, we knew we'd have to devote a fair amount of time to get around it. Yet every summer had mostly been spent at a ballpark.

Until the summer of 2011, that is.

That's when we took off, throwing ourselves wholly into the experience. I can't think of a time when I'd left my business for two full weeks (although I squeezed in a business event by attending the National Speakers Association conference in Anaheim). Before leaving, I notified clients, delegated duties to my virtual assistant, and didn't look back.

Sorry, Facebook friends, I didn't post "in the moment" pictures of us walking across the Golden Gate Bridge, nor did I share with you the awe and beauty of the Sequoias or the incredible falls of Yosemite. I didn't post my exuberance over white water rafting for the first time, nor did I share my reactions to the quirkiness of Venice Beach or the magnificence of Big Sur Drive. Those experiences were just for us. And we truly lived "in the moment."

> *You see, **disconnecting** from my office, from social media, and from 24/7 accessibility, allowed me to fully **reconnect** with the loved ones in my family—my top priority.*

As I was growing up, we often went to our "camp" at Grand Isle. Back then, my daddy would take two consecutive weeks of vacation and we'd spend every minute of it at Grand Isle. This meant being cut off from the rest of the world—well, except for the people there. On Grand Isle, we had no phone, no cable TV, and certainly no cell phones. Being completely unplugged felt totally relaxing!

But with today's 24/7 connectivity, I'd never unplugged like that since I was a kid. Until our California vacation.

Proudly Unplugged

Looking back, I'm proud that I allowed myself to unplug this time. I didn't bring my laptop or check emails or call the office to pick up voice messages. And I didn't feel guilty, either. Unplugging was a special "something" I did for myself, my family—and for my clients.

You see, *disconnecting* from my office, from social media, and from 24/7 accessibility, allowed me to fully *reconnect* with the loved ones in my family—my top priority.

It's not that I don't value my clients. I do. But from working with me, they know how strongly I feel about honoring my priorities. That's why I value them so much; they "get" me and I "get" them.

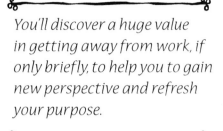

You'll discover a huge value in getting away from work, if only briefly, to help you to gain new perspective and refresh your purpose.

Having allowed myself to unplug and recharge enabled me to give better service to my clients when I returned to work. And the same holds true for any leader.

Can you unplug so that you can be of better service to your team? You may not be able to take off for two weeks, but have you considered fully disconnecting even for a few days? I know leaders who go on a weeklong vacation but constantly field calls, emails, and text messages. How can you relax on a beach somewhere but hardly see its beauty because you're texting, emailing, and talking on the phone? That just wouldn't cut it for me.

You'll discover a huge value in getting away from work, if only briefly, to help you to gain new perspective and refresh your purpose. Watch your team members benefit, too. Train someone to cover for you during your absence. You'll come back rejuvenated, and that team member will have gained a dose of confidence and self-assurance in the process.

Now that I feel recharged, please excuse me. I have to get back to work.

Ain't Dere No More

To lament the 2005 loss of local iconic New Orleans stores, businesses, and restaurants, local singer/songwriter Benny Grunch and the Bunch popularized the phrase "Ain't Dere No More."

Ain't dere no more, indeed. Hurricane Katrina gave tremendous new meaning to the concept of adapting to change. One phrase repeated often was the "new normal," as in "Yeah, we're makin' it. Dealin' with the new normal."

Still, years later, people in this state are asking, "Who Moved My . . . World?"

Who Moved My World?

In the summer and fall of 2005 when not one but two major natural hurricanes hit Louisiana (Hurricane Rita followed Hurricane Katrina about a month later), the word "change" became a gross understatement.

Thousands had their entire worlds turned upside down. Countless victims lost their homes, businesses, jobs, and, sadly, loved ones. I say this not to state the obvious but because I don't want to minimize the devastating losses many people experienced.

While my hometown of Thibodaux was blessedly spared the degree of destruction that hit New Orleans and the Gulf Coast, we faced changes, too. In a small way, I experienced a type of survivor's guilt laced with depression—something that happens when people who escape unscathed from a tragedy feel guilty because they survived while others next to them perished.

During the weeks after the storms, slowly but surely, I made contact with friends from the devastated areas. I found one friend looking for job opportunities in Virginia and then in North Carolina, where he ultimately settled. Another friend set up shop (and home and school) in Houston. One permanently relocated from the Lakeview area to Baton Rouge. Others were strewn throughout the 50 states, unsure what their futures would hold—and where.

> *Our state's business climate had to adjust to a "new normal." As long-time clients disappeared, brand new opportunities had to be created.*

The storms not only rearranged the lives of those who were hit physically. Our state's business climate had to adjust to a "new normal." As long-time clients disappeared, brand new opportunities had to be created. Bravely, leaders within organizations played an important role in helping employees make unanticipated shifts.

Who Moved My Cheese?

The parable of *Who Moved My Cheese: An Amazing Way to Deal with Change in Your Work and in Your Life* by Spencer Johnson[15] provides a reality check for people whose lives face upheaval. Its four characters—two mice (Sniff and Scurry) and two "little people" (Hem and Haw)—live in a maze and search for cheese every day to survive. (The cheese represents anything people chase that they believe will make them happy.)

The characters get used to finding a big cache of cheese in one spot—until one day, the cheese isn't there anymore. Sound familiar? Sniff and Scurry immediately disperse to find new cheese while

Hem and Haw freak out and worry and waste a whole lot of time.

This parable reminds us to be alert to changes so we don't get caught unprepared when our cheese (or job, customer, business, client, etc.) inevitably disappears. At times of great change, leaders especially need to take care of business instead of Hemming and Hawing or getting bogged down in overanalyzing the situation.

Talking about the epic changes experienced with Hurricane Katrina, adjusting is a whole lot easier said than done. I heard one TV commentator say that, in these circumstances, doing what needs to be done while keeping an organization running is akin to rebuilding an airplane's engines while flying it at 10,000 feet!

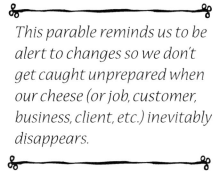

This parable reminds us to be alert to changes so we don't get caught unprepared when our cheese (or job, customer, business, client, etc.) inevitably disappears.

And When the Cheese Disappears . . .

As a leader, what's your first job when the cheese disappears? To pull your team together and get clear about *where* you're heading and *why*. In fact, all personal, team, or organizational change begins with this approach. It's called "imagineering"—a term Walt Disney coined—that mixes engineering skills with imagination to creatively develop your organization's vision.

I suggest using change opportunities to "imagineer" your organization anew without the problems and flaws you've experienced before. Get everyone moving in the same direction with a shared vision of your organization's "new normal," then align every action with this vision. Make sure all team members understand their new roles and direct their energies toward the company's vision every day.

Aldous Huxley said, "Experience is not what happens to a man; it is what a man does with what happens to him." Yes, the events of 2005 dramatically affected us. Each person chose how to respond to those events. I hope they focused on coming out of the storm better for it!

It is my fervent prayer that you'll never have to face change in such dramatic or catastrophic proportions as South Louisiana did. Still, you *will* be bombarded with significant shifts.

What will you do when you face easier-said-than-done opportunities? Will you Hem and Haw and waste a whole lot of time? Or will you Sniff and Scurry and lead your team to find the "cheese" in new places?

Ultimately, the choice is yours.

Mardi Gras, Lent, and Leadership

New Orleans and South Louisiana are known for their lavish Mardi Gras, or Fat Tuesday, celebrations. Mardi Gras Day marks the culmination of the Mardi Gras season, which officially begins on Twelfth Night, January 6, each year. This time for revelry and often indulgence runs until the day before Ash Wednesday, which marks the start of the austere, reflective time of Lent.

Regardless of your religion or beliefs, leadership lessons abound in these traditions.

Although folks in South Louisiana typically need no excuse for a party, Mardi Gras provides a time for everyone to come together, forget their differences, and celebrate with *joie de vivre*. Everyone enjoys a festive mood and loves to share in the celebration, hence the common expression, *laissez les bons temps roulez!* (Let the good times roll!).

> *There's a strong business case for bringing more fun into your environment. What ways can you jazz up your workplace and celebrate life?*

The Festive Season of Mardi Gras

Now, I'm not suggesting you throw a parade or host a huge Mardi Gras tableau in your workplace. Yours is a serious business. But can you at least create opportunities for celebration, lightheartedness, and *joie de vivre* as part of your business, too?

If the nature of your work seems too serious to have festivities, well, that's all the more reason you *need* to bring them in. Think about the medics who treat cancer patients and terminally ill children—grim, depressing work if they never have opportunities to lighten up. Certainly their patients don't benefit from having caregivers who are grim and depressed. Rather, they're better off around people who feel upbeat and positive.

It may sound counterintuitive, but it's crucial to slow down in order to speed up toward increased productivity, innovation, and problem solving.

And your work might not need to be as serious as you're making it. I'm just sayin'. . . .

Research shows that people who enjoy their work environment are more engaged, have fewer accidents, provide better customer service, and have more loyalty than those who don't. There's a strong business case for bringing more fun into your environment. What ways can you jazz up your workplace and celebrate life?

The Reflective Season of Lent

Mardi Gras is the time of revelry before the somber, austere season of Lent when people pause in introspection. It begs the question, "How often do you pause to step back and reflect?"

As a leader, it's your responsibility to take the long view, to look back and see where your organization has been and where you want it to go—a top-of-the-hill view. Plenty of people get the view from the foxhole; it's up to you to climb that hill.

After every leadership retreat or training program that I facilitate, I conduct a post mortem in which I review the feedback and consider what improvements to make in my programs. I ask my client for their feedback as well. In this way, I'm always refining my content and delivery. Without this time for reflection—my season of Lent—I couldn't continue to get better for myself and my clients.

I suggest you also take time to think about lessons you've learned, view them from the top of the hill, and plan for improvements in the future.

It may sound counterintuitive, but it's crucial to slow down in order to speed up toward increased productivity, innovation, and problem solving. By stepping back, you move forward. And by celebrating, you enjoy the journey.

Cajun Revival!

Here in South Louisiana, you can tell just by looking at my yard when the summer heat has arrived in full force. With severe drought and daily temps in the 90s, my grass looks, well, bedraggled. Since I've begun a daily watering campaign, though, the grass has perked up. I'm seeing less brown and more green every day.

Work teams can suffer from the same ailment without having anything to do with the summer heat. Daily activities can become boring, stressful, or unchallenging. After being in the same job for years, team members can get as burnt out and faded as my bedraggled grass. If people on your team have the blahs, it's your job as a leader to revive them.

Fais Do Do!

The people of South Louisiana need no excuse for a party or celebration. Back in the day, after a week of hard work, folks used to have a *fais do do* (a neighborhood dance) every Saturday night. The whole family would attend the *fais do do*—adults, children, teens, and grandparents—complete with lots of drinking, dancing, food, and fun.

The term *fais do do* actually means "go to sleep." Why would a neighborhood dance be given such a name? Well, remember, the whole family attended and this party typically went on until the wee hours of the morning. Mothers brought their infants and small children and put them to sleep in another room. To this day, the term *fais do do* is still used to refer to a Cajun dance (and we still tell our children to "go make do do," or go to sleep).

Boucherie

Another Cajun tradition is the *boucherie,* or butchering of hogs. This tradition began long ago when families and communities came together to butcher their hogs so they'd have meat for the holidays and for the rest of the winter. So of course the *boucherie* became a big celebration, with music and good food, each individual contributing their special skills and knowledge to the process.

Nothing went to waste from the pig. Cajuns used everything but the squeal!

Ways to Revitalize Your Team

What are some ways you can bring that spirit of *laissez les bon temps roulez* (let the good times roll) into your work environment?

They say that familiarity breeds contempt. The word "contempt" might be a bit strong, but I agree that familiarity can breed apathy, cynicism, irritation, impatience, and intolerance. When you've worked with the same people for a while, you can start to take their contributions for granted, even become annoyed with their quirks and habits. As in any relationship, people need to be reminded of the value they bring to the whole.

You can revitalize people without spending a lot of green (dollars). Experiment with the following ideas.

Bring fun into the workplace. This could be in the form of po-boys or pizza delivered for lunch, a weekly drawing for prizes, a football pool, awards for "catching someone doing something right," or playful prizes for doing something silly or embarrassing.

Hold friendly contests. Maybe riff off of a popular reality TV show with proceeds going to a charitable cause. Put together a competitive team (sports, trivia, etc.). Celebrate birthdays, anniversaries, and accomplishments. Sponsor themed dress days or casual dress days to introduce lightheartedness into your work environment.

Tell team members how they're making a difference. Remind them how their contributions count toward the greater good.

Thank, recognize, and praise people every chance you get. One manager I know keeps on hand lots of gift cards to popular retail stores. He can promptly reward a team member whose performance shines by giving a gift card on the spot.

When you've worked with the same people for a while, you can start to take their contributions for granted, even become annoyed with their quirks and habits. As in any relationship, people need to be reminded of the value they bring to the whole.

Encourage employees to take time off to rest, relax, and recharge their batteries. Whenever possible, allow them to unplug and recharge.

Schedule a team retreat. In these retreats, team members come together to understand and appreciate each other better. They're best held away from work with a professional facilitator, perhaps meals and refreshments included. (I work with many organizations in this capacity and can explain firsthand the long-term benefits of holding retreats. Schedule one for your team. No, this does not mean holding hands and singing "Kumbaya"; maybe "We Are the World" instead!)

Provide growth opportunities. Give your team members

challenging responsibilities by allowing them to cross-train, take professional development classes, or learn a new skill that interests them.

Revitalizing your team is like having a daily watering campaign rejuvenating my green grass. *Laissez les bons temps roulez!*

Leadership Lagniappe

Pick up more ideas on how to add more zest while
Optimizing Your Influence at:

http://www.ledetmanagement.com/freeresources

Epilogue: Laissez Faire

Well, you finally get to eat the gumbo! I hope you've enjoyed visiting with me as you followed my GUMBO recipe for great leadership.

Remember the expression I shared with you at the beginning of this book? "No two gumbos are alike, and nobody's gumbo's as good as your mama's!"

You'll surely find that you can adapt my gumbo recipe and add your own flavor to it. Your dish will be different from mine—that's what good Cajun cooking's all about. When I go into the kitchen to cook a gumbo (or anything, really), I don't use a recipe. I put a little of this, a little of that, and just see how it comes out. I learned to cook by trial and error and, believe me, I'm still learning!

What I've learned from my Cajun heritage, though, is that the most important ingredients in any dish are *heart and soul.*

Once you've mastered the basic ingredients of your leadership GUMBO, you'll want to add your own flavor, style, and heart and soul. You, too, will learn through trial and error, but the most important part is to learn from your mistakes.

The French expression *laissez faire* means to let people do as they choose. Lao Tzu's wisdom regarding humility in leadership applies here: "A leader is best when people barely know he exists; when his work is done, his aim fulfilled, they will say: we did it ourselves." So once you've learned and mastered this leadership GUMBO recipe, it's time to back off a bit and practice *laissez faire.*

Whether you're a Cajun from down the bayou or a Yankee (we call people Yankees if they're not from here, whether they're from North Dakota or North Louisiana!), I encourage you to make your own strong GUMBO recipe for success.

Thank you for walking through this leadership model with me. I've shared my own experiences with you and ask you to share your stories of great GUMBO with me.

Leadership Lagniappe
Go Further!

Dig deeper into this important topic as we
continue the conversation on my blog at
www.LedetManagement.com.
Keep in touch. Tell me how this book has helped you
develop your own recipe for success. There, you can
post comments, pose questions, and ask for advice on
your specific leadership issues.

Mae cher, I hope to see ya'll there soon!

About the Author

Born and raised along the bayous of South Louisiana, Jennifer Ledet loves to spice up her leadership and employee engagement work with Cajun-style wisdom.

Armed with a background in human resources management and blessed with a passion for people, Jennifer assists leaders—from VPs and CEOs to front-line supervisors and managers — build relationships and improve influence to impact the bottom line.

In her keynote presentations, leadership retreats, and team-building workshops, Jennifer's warm down-home personality gets participants energized and inspired to make changes—that create lasting results.

Jennifer continues to live in the heart of bayou country with her husband Steve, their children Lauren, Justin, and Philip, and their dog Tabasco.

Acknowledgments

This book would not have been possible without a lot of help and support. I'd like to humbly thank the following people for their contributions and encouragement:

Thank you to my many clients for making me a partner in your businesses and for putting your trust in me. It has been my honor and privilege to know you, work with you, learn from you, and grow with you. I look forward to many more years together!

I am grateful to my friends, colleagues, and mentors as well as to my role models and coaches in the National Speakers Association. Thank you for so generously and graciously sharing your knowledge, your time, and your expertise. I only pray that I can someday return the favor, and I will always do my best to pay it forward.

I'm so appreciative to my rich and flavorful Cajun heritage. I'm thankful that I was born and raised in God's Country. I wouldn't want to live anywhere else in the world.

I'm eternally thankful to my mama and daddy for giving me my love of reading and lifelong learning (Mama) and for my insatiable curiosity and determination (Daddy).

I can't express enough my gratitude to Lauren, Justin, and Philip. Thank you for giving me my inspiration and my "why" for doing meaningful work. I'm now making valuable contributions to the business world . . . on my terms. I'd gladly chuck it all again to stay home and be your mama. I'm so proud of each of you and love you "big as the world."

And last, but certainly not least, I give my thanks to my husband Steve for your patience, and understanding, support, and belief in me. You have always been my biggest cheerleader and I couldn't do any of what I do without you. I love you MORE!

Endnotes

1   Bob Hamm. "What is a Cajun?" *Cajun Nursery Rhymes Book II*. Prime Time Enterprises Publishing Division. 2000. p. 1.

2   Marcus Buckingham. *Now, Discover Your Strengths*. The Gallup Organization. 2001.

3   http://www.care2.com/c2c/groups/disc.html?gpp=10215&pst=1294716

4   http://www.louisianatravel.com/roots-cajun-culture

5   http://eqi.org/eidefs.htm

6   Travis Bradberry and Jean Greaves. *Emotional Intelligence 2.0*. TalentSmart. 2009.

7   Louisiana Office of Lieutenant Governor: http://www.crt.state.la.us/ltgovernor/

8   Marshall Goldsmith. *What Got You Here Won't Get You There*. Hyperion Books. 2007.

9   http://ezinearticles.com/?When-Personalities-Clash-at-the-Workplace&id=6317994

10   Robert L. Fulghum. *All I Really Need to Know I Learned in Kindergarten*. Ballantine Books. 1986. pp.1-3.

11   Dale Carnegie. *How to Win Friends and Influence People*. Simon and Schuster. 1936.

12   Rudy M. Yandrick. "Workplace Bullying Can Cause High Turnover, Low Productivity and Decreased Morale," *HR Magazine*. Oct 1, 1999.

13 Laurence J. Peter, Raymond Hull. *The Peter Principle: Why Things Always Go Wrong.* William Morrow and Company. 1969.

14 Bob Hamm. Passage from the poem "A Cajun Welcome." www.whatisacajun.com.

15 Spencer Johnson. *Who Moved My Cheese: An Amazing Way to Deal with Change in Your Work and in Your Life.* G. P. Putnam's Sons. 1998.

CPSIA information can be obtained at www.ICGtesting.com
Printed in the USA
LVOW120109170512

282105LV00005B/4/P